The Annuity Stanifesto

Stan G. Haithcock

Published by
AnnuityMan Publishing
Ponte Vedra Beach, Florida

ISBN: 0615895514
ISBN 13: 9780615895512
LCCN: 2013920069
AnnuityMan Publishing, Ponte Vedra Beach, FL

Timeless Quotes **& Stanisms**

"Own an annuity for what it *will do*, not what it might do."
Stan The Annuity Man

"If it sounds too good to be true, then it is. No exceptions."
Somebody Really Smart

"Buying an annuity for an up-front bonus is like buying a car for the stereo."
Stan The Annuity Man

"Life is hard. Life is harder when you're stupid."
John Wayne

"When it comes to annuities…don't buy the sizzle, buy the steak."
Stan The Annuity Man

"True simplicity is very complex and hard to achieve."
Steve Jobs

"When the going gets weird…the weird turn pro."
Hunter S. Thompson

"When you go to a bad chicken dinner annuity seminar, make sure to only swallow the food, not the sales pitch."
Stan The Annuity Man

"There are no U-Hauls behind hearses."
Unknown Visionary

"Not using an income rider that is attached to your annuity is like having a Corvette parked in your garage and never driving it."
Stan The Annuity Man

"Annuities are transfer of risk strategies and should only be owned for their contractual guarantees."
Stan The Annuity Man

Preface

When I first started writing this book a few years ago and offered parts of it as a PDF download on my website, I thought that might be it for me as an author. *The Annuity Stanifesto* reflects the way my brain and personality work—succinct and to the point. My goal was to create an easy-to-read "annuity primer" that would serve as a simple resource for people who needed to find out the real facts about all things annuity.

As I have traveled the country, I have been described as an annuity ambassador and a national annuity consumer advocate. I do consider myself The Annuity Critic™, and I always enjoy speaking to people and showing them the proper ways to use an annuity within their specific portfolio.

Over the past few years, I have developed my own unique annuity strategies and have learned how to explain different annuity products and solutions so that anyone can understand how these sometimes complex products work. I have literally been asked thousands of times for copies of my PowerPoint presentations or yellow pad scribblings that explain specific strategies.

As my client base has grown across the country and my national annuity workshops keep getting larger and larger, the requests for my presentations "in book form" have finally pushed me to sit down and finish writing the final parts of *The Annuity Stanifesto* for the sole purpose of helping the public understand the numerous ways that annuities can help contractually solve problems.

I hope that this book achieves the goal of "annuity simplicity." If it does, then I deem it a success.

Acknowledgments

When I burnt the boat by deciding to focus only on annuities and become Stan The Annuity Man®, I would have never dreamed how this "Annuity Man project" would have grown. Today I look forward to never retiring...working until the very end...and always being Stan The Annuity Man. I would like to thank many people who have supported the company and character that is Stan The Annuity Man. You know who you are, and if I happened to omit you from the list below, I apologize. I really appreciate everything that all of you have done in this crazy journey, and I look forward to a fun and unpredictable future.

Thanks to my family...my wonderful wife, Christine; my lovely daughters, Brielle and Brenna; Cutie, the Wonderdog Shih Tzu; my parents, Tee and Faye (the coaches!); and my sister, Teemi.

Also, thanks and kudos to: Leah Brandt, Todd Maroney, and Jennifer Grissom for their time, efforts, and talents in helping me with *The Annuity Stanifesto*.

Additional thanks to Jim Farrish, Owen Schrum, Bill Black, Ron Webb, Dick Hickory, David Reeves, Greg Lowder, Glenn Yarbrough, Uncle Larry (rest in peace), Steve Stern, Darren Wiseman, Brian Biwer, Brad Franz, Joe Simonds, Jeff Lunn, Cheryl Meide, Craig Cerrana, Carrie Martz, and of course my honorary board members and personal icons, "Pistol" Pete Maravich and Steve Jobs.

Letter to the **Annuity Industry**

Let me get on my soapbox for a little bit about the current state of annuities. The annuity industry needs to do some self-cleaning in my opinion. The fact is that too many annuity buyers do not really know what they own. Agents need to stop selling income riders as yield, or variable annuities or indexed annuities, as the best things ever. The "bad chicken dinner" seminars need to stop; the one-product-fits-all sales strategies have to end.

Annuities are fantastic transfer of risk products that should be customized for every individual situation. The annuity industry needs to do a better job of educating the public on how these products work. The decision to own an annuity should be based on the contractual guarantees within the policy, not hypothetical or projected returns.

Stop rewarding agents for the quantity of a specific product that they sell. Stop pushing the highest commission and highest fee products. The public is eventually going to demand simplicity, transparency, and agent responsibility. I am proud to be an annuity specialist and a nationally recognized annuity expert, but I am embarrassed to see that too many annuities are improperly sold.

In the future, my hope is that more and more annuities will be sold directly to the consumer. Yes, that will probably hurt or possibly eliminate my business, and I'm OK with that. In fact, I hope to be a leader and a pioneer in this direct-to-consumer transition.

It's time for the annuity industry to wake up, clean it up, and start reversing the bad reputation it has unfortunately earned.

INTRODUCTION

There are trillions of dollars in annuities held in the United States, and that amount grows by an estimated $200 billion annually. There's a big problem with these numbers because too many people who own annuities don't really know what they own or why they own it—other than the fact that an agent or advisor said they needed one.

The first financial contracts resembling annuities were developed in ancient Roman times. Later they were also very popular in France during the seventeenth century. These first annuity structures were designed to provide a lifetime "pension type" income stream, similar to today's Single Premium Immediate Annuity structure. For over two centuries, annuities have been available in some form in the United States.

Annuities get a bad rap, and most of it is well deserved. The "bad chicken dinner" seminars, the "too good to be true" sales pitch, or the trusted advisor who all of a sudden wants to put a large portion—or even *all*—of your assets into a variable or indexed annuity have become common conduits to annuity ownership. Yes, the annuity industry has earned its bad reputation.

Annuities are in essence contractual guarantees. That is how they should be considered—and in a perfect world, sold. When you are considering an annuity for your portfolio, ask yourself two initial questions to determine if you even need an annuity solution:

1. What specific goal or problem am I looking to solve, and what do I want the money to do?
2. Will the contractual guarantees within that policy solve that specific goal or problem?

The Annuity Stanifesto is designed to help you assess your need for a possible transfer of risk strategy using an annuity to solve for principal protection, income for life, legacy, or long-term/ confinement care. When making a decision to purchase an annuity, it's important to remember that you should own an annuity for what it *will do* (contractual guarantees), not what it *might do* (hypothetical returns).

STAN THE ANNUITY MAN®

Who Is **Stan The Annuity Man®?**

My journey to becoming Stan The Annuity Man® is a pretty interesting story. Basketball was the most important thing in my life for a long time because both of my parents were coaches. Ironically, I really don't care about the game at all now. I grew up in North Carolina (a basketball hotbed), and, with my father's guidance coming from his college coaching experience, I was able to fully pay for college because I could really shoot the basketball. I finished my basketball career at the University of Central Florida, where I hold one record: the single-season free throw percentage record, of 92 percent. Big deal, huh? Not. My fascination with Wall Street and investing has always been a driving force in my life, and I have been in the financial services industry ever since I graduated from college.

During my career, I worked for many well-known Wall Street firms such as Dean Witter, Morgan Stanley, PaineWebber, and UBS. After PaineWebber was purchased by UBS, I made a decision to leave the wirehouse world and focus solely on annuities on a national basis. I learned a lot working for those brokerage firms and had some great mentors and partners along the way who taught me about portfolio management and the markets in general. That investment management experience is the foundation that I feel helps me implement annuities correctly within someone's portfolio.

Unlike most agents who sell annuities, I actually have managed money before—in the real world and at a very high level. I decided to leave Wall Street and become Stan The Annuity Man because I am a born contrarian. I felt the need for a go-to person whom people can trust to tell the truth about annuities. I want to be that person. That is the primary goal of my company, Stan The Annuity Man. I am fortunate to have client relationships in almost every state and to independently represent the best annuity carriers in the country.

The Annuity Stanifesto ... Really?

The Merriam-Webster dictionary defines the word "manifesto" as "a written statement declaring publicly the intentions, motives, or views of the issuer." *The Annuity Stanifesto* is a synopsis of my views on the world of annuities that describes how these sometimes controversial products should be properly used within a portfolio. I wrote it because the public needs to know the truth and the facts about annuities.

Mission Statement

My goal is to find the right annuity solution with the right annuity company to contractually solve your specific goals. I would also like to help educate people on the world of annuities, how they work, and to become the premier national consumer advocate for annuities, while remaining an objective and outspoken resource as The Annuity Critic™ for the country.

Every customized annuity plan that I put together is based solely on the contractual guarantees that the policy provides— in other words, the worst-case scenario. As I always tell my clients, you own an annuity for what it *will do,* not what it *might do.*

Why I Burnt the Boat

I decided to focus solely on annuities on a national basis because too many annuities are sold improperly and are not positioned correctly within a portfolio. I want to continually educate the public on how annuities work and how they can contractually help your specific situation.

TABLE OF CONTENTS

PART I

STANNUITY FACTS

The History of Annuities

‖‖

Most historians agree that the Romans were first to develop annuities, but some financial archaeologists argue that annuities actually existed in Egypt from 2000 to 1700 BC when a prince from a place called Sint in the Middle Kingdom created the first annuity payment plan. Perhaps annuities could have been called "sints."

In Rome, annuity solutions for Roman citizens were designed as simple lifetime income strategies for the entire family. Those early strategies became the genesis for today's Single Premium Immediate Annuity (SPIA), also known as an income annuity.

For the annuity-loving Romans, the Latin word *annua* actually meant annual payments. Obviously, that's how the word annuity was derived.

Roman soldiers were paid annuity lifetime payments in compensation for their military service to the empire. Back then—and in fact up to 1952 when the first variable annuity was introduced—the only annuity structure and strategy available was the SPIA—the original design, and in my opinion, still the most pro-consumer annuity available. In addition to being called income annuities, SPIAs are sometimes referred to as pension annuities.

It is interesting to look back at how the annuity category has grown since the Romans started it all, particularly the developments of the past couple hundred years.

1600s — European governments started to use annuity-like strategies to pay for wars and public works projects. Early individual annuity structures were called "tontines." These strategies were "life only" annuity payments to a family, with the lifetime income actually increasing to surviving family members. Sounds like a pretty good deal.

1700s — After the British Parliament approved annuity sales to the public, the British elite and other rich Europeans began to use annuities as transfer of risk strategies, often to hedge riskier investments. Those Brits were pretty smart, because that is still a great way to use annuities within a portfolio.

1759 — The first annuities to be offered in America were fixed annuities that were structured as a lifetime retirement payment plan for church pastors in the great state of Pennsylvania.

1776 — The National Pension Program for Soldiers was approved and passed even before the Declaration of Independence was signed. Wow! These early annuity products provided lifetime income payments to soldiers and their families.

1812 — With the founding of The Pennsylvania Company for the Granting of Annuities, commercial annuities became available to the public at large for the first time. Way to go Pennsylvania!

1905 — All-around genius and philanthropist Andrew Carnegie founded the Teachers Pension Fund, which offered teachers pension-like annuity payments.

1918 — The Teachers Pension Fund became the Teachers Insurance Annuity Association (TIAA). Educators still benefit from annuity offerings through that same company, now known as TIAA-CREF.

1930s — When the Great Depression devastated the markets and the economy, investors started turning to annuities as a safe haven from volatile markets. Sound familiar? The "safe haven" annuity strategy should not be forgotten.

1952 — The first deferred variable annuity was introduced by TIAA-CREF. By the way, the "CREF" of TIAA-CREF stands for College Retirement Equities Fund.

1964 — Stan Haithcock was born in Milford, Delaware, and was named by his father after Hall of

Fame baseball player Stan "The Man" Musial. In a glimpse into the future and in true contrarian form, Stan made basketball instead of baseball his sport of choice. This young man would eventually change the financial world by becoming Stan The Annuity Man®.

1986 — Congress actually did something right by passing a tax law that allowed people to benefit from tax-deferred growth using annuities. Fortunately, they placed no limitations on the amount of money that could take advantage of this tax deferral strategy.

1995 — The first Fixed Index Annuity was offered by Keyport (eventually purchased by Sun Life). This also could be the beginning of the bad chicken dinner annuity seminar!

2003 — Income riders were first introduced as guaranteed income benefits that could be attached to variable annuities. A few years later, income riders attached to fixed annuities and fixed index annuities became available. These contractual income benefits gained new popularity after the stock market volatility in 2008.

2004 — The first Longevity Annuity—also called a "Deferred Income Annuity"—was introduced by MetLife. Sales of this efficient "Income Later" strategy didn't start catching on until 2010, when large and well-respected carriers like New York Life and Guardian began to offer this fantastic product.

2006 — An experienced wealth advisor with a major Wall Street firm decides to leave and start his own company to focus only on annuities. Eventually becoming a recognized expert and critic on the subject, he has been frequently called The National Consumer Advocate for Annuities. Focusing only on contractual guarantees and the factual truths about annuities, he calls himself and his new company Stan The Annuity Man®.

2014 – *The Annuity Stanifesto* is published, forever changing the way annuities are bought, sold, explained, and understood.

How and Where Annuities Work in Your Portfolio

Transfer the Risk

Annuities should be used as transfer of risk solutions within your portfolio. In essence, you are transferring the risk to the insurance company instead of shouldering it yourself. The older you are, the more transfer of risk assets you need to provide coverage for issues like lifetime income or long-term care. I always advise people to see how much risk in their total portfolios they are currently shouldering and how much risk they have transferred. Most people are alarmed by how little risk they have transferred.

Annuities should solve for only four problems within your portfolio. An-easy-to-remember acronym I came up with is the word PILL©.

P.I.L.L.©: What Annuities Should Solve For

P rincipal Protection

I ncome for Life

L egacy

L ong Term Care/Confinement Care

P = Principal Protection

In a world of low interest rates, it has been a tough few years for the savers and depositors. You can only get real principal protection in five places:

1. CDs (up to FDIC limit rules)

2. Money Market (up to FDIC limit rules)

3. Municipal Bonds (insured)

4. Treasuries

5. Fixed Annuities (with strong carriers)

Fixed Annuities are backed by the full faith and credit of the issuing carrier, and each state has a guaranty fund that backs each policy up to a certain dollar amount (each state's coverage is described at www.nolhga.com). State guaranty funds should not be compared with FDIC type coverage, and they should not be a consideration when purchasing an annuity.

An annuity guarantee is only as good as the issuing company, so 100 percent of your buying decision should revolve around that company's ability to stand behind those contractual promises.

Insurance companies and annuities are "confidence" products, and the industry self-regulates pretty effectively. Also, with annuities being regulated at the state level, the capital requirements in place for insurance companies are much more stringent than they are for banks.

I = Income for Life

If you are fortunate enough to be receiving pension payments from a previous employer, you already have an annuity income stream type of payment. If you receive a Social Security check, that is an annuity income stream type of payment as well. However, you might need more guaranteed income, or you might be afraid of outliving your money (what we call "longevity risk"). Here is where income annuities can possibly complement your portfolio.

Annuities were initially developed for income, and in most cases, lifetime income. There are two primary ways to use annuities for income planning:

  1. Income Now or Immediate Income

  2. Income Later or Target Date Income

Using only the contractual guarantees as the basis for all income planning, an annuity can provide a lifetime income stream for you (and your spouse if applicable), transferring that lifetime payment risk to the annuity company.

How Income Is Paid from an Annuity

Annuitization Method

Annuitization is the process of converting the account value of an annuity into a series of guaranteed periodic income payments. Those payments can be set up to pay monthly, quarterly, or annually. They also can be structured to pay for life, a certain period of time, or both. If structured to pay for life, payments are based on your life expectancy when the income is initially turned on. Once this option has started, it cannot be changed.

Drawdown Method

The lifetime income drawdown method is normally used with "income riders" that are attached to a deferred annuity policy. Unlike with annuitization, you have the ability to turn your income stream on or off at your discretion while retaining full control over the annuity asset. Again, payments are based on your life expectancy when the income is initially turned on.

Actuarial Rate

The Actuarial Rate—one of the most important parts of the annuity contract, as it helps determine your lifetime income payout—is a percentage of the total account value or income rider value (whichever is higher) from which the lifetime income stream payment is calculated. Based on your life expectancy, it is a transfer of risk to the annuity company to pay you for the rest of your life, regardless of how long you live. Some annuities have what I call "banded rates," which means that, for example, from age sixty to sixty-five a certain percentage is applied, from sixty-six to seventy a higher percentage is applied, and so on.

Other annuities apply actuarial calculations to the age you are when you choose to turn on the income stream. It goes without saying that you should know which one of these actuarial calculation methods you own or are considering owning and which one provides the highest contractual guarantee. It's also important to point out that any income riders (attached income benefit) on fixed annuities normally have higher actuarial payout rates than that same income rider if attached to variable annuities. For this reason, I always recommend income riders on fixed annuities and consider deferred annuities as nothing more than a delivery system for income riders when they are appropriate and suitable for Income Later strategies.

Basic Income Strategies

Immediate (Income Now)

Immediate income needs, or what I call Income Now, are what the original annuity was strategically designed to provide. Immediate Annuities (also called Single Premium Immediate Annuities or Income Annuities) start your lifetime income stream one month from the contract issue date. Immediate Annuities can be structured for one or two lives, for a specific period of time, or both lives with a guaranteed minimum period. Income Now quotes are a true commodity, and I always list the highest contractual guaranteed payments of the top five to ten different carriers based on your age or ages.

Target Date (Income Later)

If you need income down the road at a date in the future, two annuity strategies can provide the contractual guarantees to help with your retirement income planning. Regardless of when you plan on starting your lifetime income stream, these Target Date (Income Later) annuity strategies allow you to calculate to the penny what your contractually guaranteed payments will be. You can use Income Later annuity strategies with income riders, benefits attached to your deferred annuity contract, or with Longevity Annuities (also called Deferred Income Annuities). When I run contractually guaranteed Income Later proposals for my clients, I always show both strategies and fully explain how they work so that they can make informed decisions.

Deferred Income Delivery Systems© (DIDS)

Because I only look at the contractual guarantees of a policy, I consider deferred annuities like variable or in-dexed nothing more than delivery systems for the in-come rider–guaranteed growth calculations and payouts. Deferred Income Delivery Systems© (DIDS), a Stan The Annuity Man original term, arose from the genesis of a thought I had about how drones deliver their payload: Who cares about the drone? It's about what it's carrying. The same can be said for a variable or indexed annuity with an attached income rider. Who cares about the de-ferred annuity accumulation value? It's about the income rider and the highest contractual guaranteed payout you can find for your future income needs.

Historically, income riders that are attached to fixed annuities provide higher contractual guarantees than similar income rid-ers attached to variable annuities. And yet most income riders sold today are attached to variable annuities. Why? Because people like to buy the pipe dream of all upside gains plus guarantees too. Usually that doesn't seem to work out too well. My advice is to stay in Annuity Realityville: Own an annuity for what it *will do,* not what it *might do.*

Inflation Protection

Annuities can offer some protection from inflation with annual contractual percentage increase guarantees called a COLA. COLA, which stands for Cost of Living Adjustment, is a rider you can attach to an immediate annuity (SPIA) or Longevity Annuity (DIA). COLAs provide a contractual annual increase that you can choose during the application process, normally between 3 percent to 5 percent. Other annuities offer contractual increases attached to growth in the Consumer Price Index (CPI) or the CPI–All Urban Consumers (CPI-U), a measurement of the buying habits of the large majority of Americans. Some Fixed Index Annuities (FIAs) can also increase your income stream with an attached call option strategy. Not all annuities offer inflation strategies, and when you do attach a benefit to contractually address inflation, the initial payout is typically much lower than the same annuity without an inflation increase guarantee. There is no free lunch, and there is not an annuity on the planet that will truly address hyperinflation. That's a fact.

For much more information about how COLA, CPI, CPI-U, and Index increases work with annuities to combat inflation, visit The AnnuityMan Steakhouse™ at my website.

L = Legacy

Leaving a legacy is a goal that most share. Annuities that contractually guarantee an annual growth percentage can be left to your listed beneficiaries, and some contractually grow for long periods of time. Annuity proceeds pass outside of probate, giving you an efficient way to leave some of your assets to your heirs while protecting and controlling your principal when you are alive. That said, pure life insurance is still the best legacy strategy available. I always tell people that life insurance is the best return on investment that you will never see! So annuities finish second to life insurance when it comes to legacy, and a distant second at best. Also, annuity legacy benefits do not pass tax-free to your beneficiaries as life insurance does; despite being a life insurance product, they don't share its tax benefits.

Required Minimum Distribution Strategy for Individual Retirement Accounts

Many people are fortunate to have earned and saved enough assets that they can focus mainly on how to leave as much of their money as possible to their family or designated charity. Some Fixed Annuities have been designed to be placed within an Individual Retirement Account (IRA) to combat Required Minimum Distribution (RMD) withdrawals by providing contractual growth guarantees to offset your annual RMD amount. In some situations, such an annuity contractual guarantee will allow you to leave your IRA assets intact for your beneficiaries, regardless of how many RMDs you take over your lifetime.

Look at your portfolio from a legacy standpoint. Ask yourself how much risk are you shouldering...or willing to shoulder. A contractually guaranteed Fixed Annuity strategy might be the turnkey approach that takes the worry out of your legacy planning—especially for the assets within your IRA.

Go to The AnnuityMan Steakhouse™ at my website for an example of the RMD Strategy for IRAs or to request a proposal.

Leveraged Legacy Doubler©

Another advanced strategy I use with clients looking to achieve both income and legacy simultaneously is called the Leveraged Legacy Doubler©, which combines an annuity policy and a life insurance policy to contractually maximize legacy benefits while also providing a contractually guaranteed lifetime income for the family, usually a spouse. Have a look at the Leveraged Legacy Doubler© strategy at The AnnuityMan Steakhouse™ on my website.

Stretch IRA Strategy

You don't need an annuity to "stretch" your IRA, but annuities can be used as an efficient vehicle for this strategy. Stretching your IRA means, in essence, having your beneficiaries take your RMD from your IRA over their lifetimes. For example, if a husband dies, his wife can then take annual RMDs adjusted for her life expectancy from his IRA. When the wife then dies, the children can take RMDs from their father's IRA based on their life expectancies. Likewise, if the children pass away, then the grandchildren can take RMDs from their grandfather's IRA based on their life expectancies. Clearly, it's very important to list the beneficiaries of your IRA correctly to implement a stretch strategy. Some deferred fixed annuities work very well for stretching an IRA because the asset is principal protected, and you can attach additional contractually guaranteed rider benefits to the policy as well. At The AnnuityMan Steakhouse™ on my website I offer an example of the stretch IRA strategy, which I can employ to help you realize your legacy wishes for your family.

L = Long-Term Care/ Confinement Care

Annuities can provide long-term care (LTC) type coverage while still allowing full control of the asset. In other words, if you never access or need the long-term care benefit, you retain power over your money. We all are living longer, and most of us would like to be taken care of in our own homes instead of a facility. Unlike most traditional long-term care products, LTC annuities provide such coverage without you losing control of the money. With some products, coverage can be guaranteed to issue regardless of your health status, and other LTC annuities require just a phone interview for approval. The bottom line is that annuities with long-term care type coverage allow you to retain full control your money if you do not use the benefit.

Guaranteed Issue LTC/Confinement Care Annuity

Some people cannot get coverage for preexisting health reasons, and some want to just supplement their current LTC coverage. I typically offer them Guaranteed Issue LTC/ Confinement Care coverage as an attached benefit rider to a Fixed Index Annuity (FIA) structure. Some of these riders provide LTC/Confinement Care payments that you can never outlive, whereas others only provide a period of LTC/ Confinement Care payments, normally five years. The payment stream for coverage is taxable at ordinary income levels, unlike traditional LTC products and pure LTC annuities, which offer significant tax benefits when the coverage is paid out.

Most LTC Riders—or the similar Confinement Care Riders— are promoted as income "doublers" for LTC. That means the benefit is built into an income rider, and whatever that payout amount is, it would double if you qualified for LTC/Confinement Care coverage under the terms of the policy. For example, let's say your income rider payout was $10,000 per year. When you stop being able to perform two out of the six daily functions, which are eating, bathing, dressing, toileting, transferring (walking), and continence, current studies estimate that you will live an average of three years and a maximum of seven years. Insurance companies base their actuarial calculations and benefits on these long-term care studies along with your life expectancy. When you meet two out of the six criteria that qualifies you for LTC/Confinement Care, then your annual payment would double to $20,000 per year.

Please understand that these riders can be complicated and hard to both understand and access, so do your homework on how they really work. I explain further how a Guaranteed Issue LTC/Confinement Care Annuity works at The AnnuityMan Steakhouse™ on my website.

Simplified Issue LTC Annuity

Some people may qualify for a Simplified Issue LTC Annuity, one that only requires a phone interview of normally fifteen to twenty questions, depending on the carrier. This type of annuity provides a tax-free LTC coverage payment stream. The maximum amount of money allowed in such LTC annuities is usually around $300,000 per person, with the LTC coverage being a multiple of the initial premium. For example, a $100,000 deposit into an LTC annuity might provide $300,000 of LTC coverage (i.e., a three times multiple) depending on the answers to the questions and how the annuity carrier issues the policy on your behalf. Go to The AnnuityMan Steakhouse™ at my website to see an example of a Simplified Issue LTC Annuity strategy.

The Entire World of Annuities

Two Ways to Play: Flexible or Single Premium

There are only two ways to fund an annuity. You can add funds ongoing or periodically with flexible payments, or you can fund the annuity in a one-time lump sum amount, or single premium.

Flexible Premium

Flexible premium annuities allow you to add funds to the annuity continuously, sometimes in a minimum dollar amount. Many 403(b) retirement plans offer flexible premium annuities as a way to add money on a monthly, quarterly, or annual basis. In my opinion the best flexible annuities currently available are Equity Indexed Annuities (EIAs), also call Fixed Index Annuities (FIAs).

Upside: Flexible premium annuities allow you to add money on your terms and on your schedule.

The flexible annuity structure is perfect for younger people who want principal protection along with locking in annual growth (or attached income rider growth) via an FIA structure. Some flexible annuities also offer bonuses on all premium deposits in addition to the option of adding an income rider.

Downside: The only real downside to flexible premium annuities is how few there are from which to choose. However, from a common-sense math calculation standpoint, if you put in a lump sum it would grow and compound more quickly than if you deposited the same amount but gradually over time. Another downside might be the minimum amount some carriers require you to deposit. Normally that dollar amount is small, but it might not seem small for some investors.

Stanalysis©: These flexible structures are great if your plans call for ongoing contributions, for example IRA contributions or long-range Target Date/Income Later planning. I wish more younger adults would use these vehicles for retirement planning and as a supplement to future Social Security payments. One idea for you parents and grandparents out there is to give an annual contribution to your child or grandchild to place into a flexible annuity, ensuring them some kind of a pension in the future.

Single Premium

The most common way to fund an annuity is with a one-time single premium amount. As the name implies, these annuities are created by making only one deposit. You will find single premium annuities on both the deferred and the immediate side. For example, all immediate annuities are single premium.

Upside: Most MYGAs (Fixed Rate Annuities) are single premium in structure because when the carriers know exactly how much money is going to be in the account, they can better plan the investments that support the contractual guarantees. Lump sum strategies mean the annuity carrier does not have to worry about buying bonds at different prices to support the guarantee.

Downside: As is clear in its name, the single premium structure does not allow you to make additional payments into these types of annuities. If you wanted to add more money to the same annuity strategy, you would need to purchase another policy.

Stanalysis©: When allocating money into a single premium annuity, you need to make sure that you understand and plan on the fact that funds cannot be added to the policy. It's really that simple and straightforward.

Types of Annuities

Single Premium Immediate Annuities

The original annuity design is the Single Premium Immediate Annuity (SPIA). Sometimes a SPIA will be called an "Income Annuity" or a "Pension Annuity," both of which are correct descriptions as well. A SPIA, a true transfer of risk product, comes in two basic types. A period certain, or certain only SPIA provides an income for a specified period of time. Once that period of time is over, the payments stop. The second type is a life or lifetime SPIA, which guarantees income payments for the rest of your life. Most of the time a period certain or premium return guarantee is attached to lifetime SPIAs. Such guarantees ensure that you receive the income for the period certain until the premium is returned or for your lifetime, *whichever comes last*. Your first payment will start as early as one month after the contract is issued and will continue for as long as you live if you choose a lifetime income stream when you set up the policy. The rest of this section will explore lifetime income SPIAs.

My advice is to consider structuring a SPIA contract either "Life with Cash Refund" or "Life with Installment Refund." These two structures ensure that you will receive a lifetime income stream regardless of how long you live; and upon your passing, 100 percent of the money remaining in the contract will go to your listed beneficiaries. The issuing annuity company will not keep a penny. This is a common misunderstanding people have about SPIAs, and that does not happen when the SPIA is structured properly.

SPIA income payments are based upon the annuitant's life expectancy. The issuing insurance company is on the hook to pay for as long as you live. Return (or payments) from SPIAs is a combination of principal and interest, so in a non-IRA account, the vast majority of your income stream will not be taxable. You can structure SPIAs to pay single life or joint life, and they can be used in both IRA and non-IRA accounts. You can also add a contractual Cost of Living Adjustment (COLA) Rider to a SPIA that will increase your income stream annually for life by some chosen percentage, normally 3 percent to 5 percent.

If you are in very poor health or have advanced stage cancer, you might qualify for medically underwritten SPIAs. During the underwriting process, the annuity company would have to review your medical records, but the lifetime payout might be higher if you qualify. Remember that annuity payouts are based on your life expectancy, so this process actually projects your life expectancy to be shorter, in turn creating a higher payout.

SPIAs can also be set up to increase income annually according to a consumer price index or to market variables other than the traditional COLA, but these strategies typically have lower payments initially than a basic SPIA so that the annuity company can make up for potential increases.

Upside: SPIAs have no internal fees and pay the lowest commission to the agent or advisor. All annuity commissions are "built into" the product, but SPIAs are the lowest, which is usually better for the customer. You will probably never go to a "bad chicken dinner" annuity seminar and have an agent base his product pitch on a SPIA. That alone should make SPIAs attractive to you! SPIAs are the most efficient way to create a lifetime income stream when you need income to start right now. Commonly used to cover basic expenses, SPIAs are not affected by stock market volatility at all. Among annuities, SPIAs are the truest and purest risk transfer.

Downside: Most SPIAs have no liquidity once the contract is past the free look period (see page 74). Once the income stream starts, you cannot turn it off or have access to the lump sum, so SPIAs need to be properly placed and in proportion within your portfolio to solve for lifetime income.

Stanalysis©: I love SPIAs, and my clients love them as well. They are the best bang for the buck and typically provide the highest contractual payout when you need lifetime income to start immediately. Nothing fancy here with this product…it just works. About fifty companies are truly competitive in this arena, and I pretty much represent them all. Also, SPIAs have a higher actuarial payout than any income rider that is attached to a deferred annuity. That's a fact worth knowing and remembering.

Go to The AnnuityMan Steakhouse™ at my website to see current examples of SPIAs and to request a specific proposal for your situation.

Fixed Rate Annuities

Fixed Rate Annuities function a lot like certificates of deposit (CDs), and are referred to in the industry as "Multi Year Rate Guaranteed" annuities (MYGAs). In essence, MYGAs are CDs but with tax deferral; typically they are purchased with a single premium amount of money.

MYGAs pay a specific percentage yield for a contractually certain amount of time. The main distinction between MYGAS and CDs is that with CDs you pay taxes annually on the interest earned. With MYGAs you defer the taxes on the interest until money is taken out. The interest rate compounds in a tax-deferred manner, which is important to consider when comparing products.

I advise clients that if their time horizon is more than two years, they should consider purchasing a MYGA. If your time horizon is less than two years, then you should probably place the money in a CD or money market fund. Fixed Rate Annuities typically have guaranteed rate lock-in periods of anywhere from two to ten years. As with CDs, surrender charges apply if you take all of your money out before the contract period ends, but most MYGAs allow you an annual 10 percent penalty-free withdrawal if you need some liquidity.

Upside: MYGAs have no internal fees and pay low (built-in) commissions to the agent or advisor. Typically, MYGAs will pay a higher contractual interest rate than a CD, and you benefit from deferring taxes on interest earned. With these MYGA strategies, you will know exactly what your rate and account value will be in the future, contractually guaranteed.

Downside: As with CDs, surrender penalties can be high if you want all of your money back before the specified term ends. Also, you have to pay attention to the contract because some MYGAs automatically renew—restarting the surrender charges at the end of the guarantee period—unless you proactively contact the annuity carrier to describe your intentions. The annuity agent of record should also be on top of any policy requirements or rules specific to you. Finally, some MYGA guarantee periods don't match up with the surrender periods. As with any annuity, always know what you own, how it works, and what the contractual rules in place actually are.

Stanalysis©: MYGAs are a great alternative to CDs if your time horizon is more than two years. Twenty to thirty competitive companies offer such products, and I represent and can quote the vast majority.

Go to The AnnuityMan Steakhouse™ at my website to see a current listing of the best MYGAs and to request a proposal. I update this list on a monthly basis and when there are any rate changes.

Fixed Index Annuities and Equity Indexed Annuities

Equity Indexed Annuities (EIAs) and Fixed Index Annuities (FIAs) are the same product. Most people don't know that they were actually designed to compete with CD returns, not market returns. That is a fact.

The industry prefers to call this strategy a Fixed Index Annuity (FIA), but the term Equity Indexed Annuity (EIA) is still used frequently by the financial press. A FIA is a fixed annuity structure with a call option on an index, normally the S&P 500. Some offer other index option choices on the Dow, NASDAQ, Russell, and so on; some offer a combination of them all. FIAs can also offer a fixed rate choice in addition to the index call option which is normally one year in length, but can be longer.

FIAs allow you to have limited participation in the index growth while retaining 100 percent downside protection. The upside participation is usually very limited, and any gains are typically locked in at the contract anniversary date. Once gains are credited to the account, they will not go away due to market loss, which is a good thing. If future income is desired, income riders should be attached to fixed annuity structures like FIAs (but not to Variable Annuities) because the cost structure for the rider is better for the client, and the actuarial payout guarantees are usually higher.

If you have gone to a "bad chicken dinner" annuity seminar, FIAs are probably what the agent or advisor is trying to sell you. I do not like most of the FIAs available today as a stand-alone strategy, and I primarily use them as efficient delivery mechanisms when income riders are needed. FIAs have limited growth potential, but for those who want principal protection and the possibility of rates greater than CDs, these products can be an appropriate choice.

Upside: As described above, FIAs allow you to have limited upside participation in the market with 100 percent downside protection. Another plus is having gains permanently locked in at the contract anniversary date and unable to fall below that amount. Typically there are no fees unless you attach contractual benefits such as an income rider or a death benefit rider to the policy, and usually those fees are relatively low. FIAs are a cost-efficient way to use income riders to solve for "Income Later" needs.

Downside: Currently, the upside growth FIAs see is very limited, and the vast majority of FIAs are not worth owning in my opinion unless used in conjunction with a specific income rider strategy for target date income planning. You may only lock in the limited gains, if any, at the contract anniversary date. Commissions to the agent can be high even though they are built into the product, which might be a primary reason for why some agents recommend FIAs so frequently.

Stanalysis©: Too many FIAs are sold improperly by agents and advisors who truly don't understand the product. Most do not know that FIAs were designed to compete with CD returns, not the market. The word "hybrid" is inappropriately and incorrectly used to hype and sell FIAs to people wanting to believe that they can have their cake and eat it too—something no annuity product can offer. If you shop for annuities on the Internet, you will find FIAs to be the most overly promoted product, pitched as the best thing since sliced bread. Remember: When it sounds too good to be true…it is. No exceptions.

Go to The AnnuityMan Steakhouse™ at my website to see a current list of the best income riders that can be attached to FIAs and to request a proposal. I also show how FIA option strategies can grow and lock in over time from an accumulation standpoint.

Variable Annuities

As we learned in our historic timeline, Variable Annuities (VAs) were developed in 1952 to help investors achieve pure tax-deferred growth. VAs have internal sub accounts (mutual funds) for growth and—just in the last few years—riders, or attached benefits. Such riders, however, in my opinion are better from an actuarial payout and cost standpoint when attached to FIAs instead.

Unfortunately, the majority of annuities currently sold in the United States are VAs—too often sold as a one-size-fits-all solution offering all of the upside of the stock market with guarantees attached. Here we have another case of "When it sounds too good to be true, it is…No exceptions." Sales of VAs keep rising, yet carriers keep getting out of the VA business because of the product structure's inherent risk and future promised guarantees. In fact, many annuity carriers are trying to buy back the contractual guarantees and living benefits of VAs to lessen their overall annuity portfolio risk.

> **Upside:** Of all the annuity choices available, VAs provide the most market potential upside participation. If you are a good money manager and understand mutual fund investing, then a no-load/no-fee variable annuity structure might make sense from a tax-deferred growth standpoint.

Downside: VAs typically have the highest internal fees in addition to very high agent commissions, with average annual fees of over 3 percent for the life of the policy. Once you start adding contractual benefit riders to the policy, the annuity company will usually limit your mutual fund (also called your "separate account") choices; in my opinion, that defeats the purpose of the product. Also, the actuarial percentage payouts—that is, the starting amount when you turn on your income stream—on VA income riders are usually lower than those for the same type of income riders attached to fixed annuities.

Stanalysis©: Let me start by saying that I don't look at any annuity as a growth product. To me and to most investors, pure growth means unlimited choices, unlimited flexibility, and full liquidity. There's not an annuity on the planet that offers these three important requirements for growth. If pure tax-deferred growth is the goal, then I would advise looking into no-load VA offerings with no attached riders. Because there are no commissions or surrender charges with no-load variable annuities, you will have to make the purchase without the help of an agent and direct from the carrier.

Charitable Annuities

I recommend two types of charitable annuities: the Charitable Gift Annuity (CGA), and the Charitable

Endowment Deferred Annuity™ (CEDA™). I am proud to say that the CEDA™ is a product that I personally have developed, and I currently oversee all of the distribution of the CEDA™ through my charitable nonprofit organization, Annuities for a Cause™.

Annuities are an efficient and philanthropic way to achieve a lifetime income stream while donating money to your charity of choice. Moreover, some very good tax benefits are currently available when using charitable annuity strategies. If you are thinking about implementing an income solution, then I would recommend comparing a charitable annuity solution with a commercial annuity solution. Then choose which overall guarantee best fits your specific situation.

Charitable Gift Annuity

Most charitable and nonprofit organizations offer Charitable Gift Annuity (CGA) programs as a way to fundraise while providing lifetime income streams and tax benefits to the donors. Ask your charity of choice about its CGA program to see if it would be a good direction for you to take. Colleges, universities, hospitals, foundations, and nonprofits normally offer CGA strategies.

Most CGAs are structured to create an immediate income stream, but some organizations allow you to defer that payment to a future date as well. Most nonprofits will customize your annuity plan to fit you.

> **Upside:** CGAs give you a lifetime income stream in exchange for donating your money to your charity of choice—plus, you receive a large tax deduction under IRS charitable donation rules.

Consult your CPA along with the organization's own tax experts to maximize this benefit. CGAs provide the kind of lifetime income stream you get with a SPIA or Longevity Annuity (DIA), but meanwhile you are helping the charity of your choice in the process.

Downside: CGAs typically offer no liquidity, so you have to make sure you don't need the money being allocated to this strategy. Also, the lifetime payout rate offered by a CGA might not be as high as a typical commercial SPIA or Longevity Annuity. Keep in mind that the lifetime income guarantee is backed in full by the charity alone, so check out its long-term financial stability before moving forward.

Stanalysis©: If you are considering a SPIA or Longevity Annuity (DIA) lifetime income type payout, ask your favorite charity what percentage rate it is paying and compare that with those of commercial annuity carriers. It may turn out that a CGA would be best for you and your family.

Charitable Endowment Deferred Annuity™

A Stan The Annuity Man–developed product, the Charitable Endowment Deferred Annuity™ (CEDA™) is a brand new strategy allowing a nonprofit or charity to offer an annuity to potential donors who want to keep full control of their money but also donate money without depleting their principal. Yes, it can be done, and my Annuities for a Cause™ group is helping nonprofits across the country do it! Contact me to learn more, or to have Annuities for a Cause™ help your organization raise more money using our proprietary annuity fundraising methods.

Upside: With the CEDA™, you can donate now, control your money, and then donate again by leaving the charity as a full or partial beneficiary. The CEDA™ also provides full principal protection using a fixed annuity strategy with some upside growth potential and a guaranteed death benefit that can be left in full or part to the charity. CEDA™ is also a very efficient way to transfer old annuities under the IRS-approved 1035 and direct transfer rules. The CEDA™ strategy can be a phenomenal way to truly upgrade your older annuity policy.

Downside: *No* downside for the donor and *no* downside for the charity! The CEDA™ is its own new category—a true "win-win" for both donor and charity.

Stanalysis©: I am proud to have designed and developed this product for charities, providing them another good (and unique) option to raise money. A non-profit I created, Annuities for a Cause™, works directly with charities, colleges, and 501(c)(3) organizations by teaching, consulting, and helping them raise money using annuities.

Longevity Annuities
(or Deferred Income Annuities)

A Longevity Annuity is designed to provide protection against outliving your money later in life. In other words, this strategy is an efficient solution that solves for "longevity risk." It is also known as a Deferred Income Annuity (DIA), an "Advanced Life Delayed Annuity," and "Longevity Insurance." DIAs are structured like deferred immediate annuities, requiring you to wait to start receiving a lifetime payout, usually from five to ten years but up to forty-five or as little as one year. The later you choose to begin your payments the larger they will be. Remember: All annuity lifetime income payments are based on your life expectancy at the time the income stream is turned on. In addition, you can add COLA riders to these policies that contractually increase your income stream on an annual basis.

> **Upside:** Longevity Annuities usually provide the highest payout for Target Date or Income Later planning. DIAs prevent you from running out of money later in life while keeping your premium outlay to a minimum. You can defer payout up to forty-five years, and issue ages are as low as zero—hello grandparents for legacy income planning!—for non-IRA accounts or as young as age eighteen for IRA accounts. Longevity Annuities have no annual fees, no market attachments, and full principal protection. I structure these DIA/Longevity products to contractually guarantee that 100 percent of the principal goes to the family, not the annuity company in case you pass away early in the contract. For those who need income to start at a future date, I always show clients the best contractually guaranteed Longevity Annuities along with income riders so that they can compare payout levels.

> **Downside:** Lack of liquidity. Once the annuity contract is past the "free look" period, you cannot access the principal in a lump sum with most policies.

Although 100 percent of the principal is fully protected, it can be accessed only through the contractual payments. Therefore it's important in planning
to keep in mind liquidity limitations and allocate the
appropriate dollar amount to this solution.

Stanalysis©: Longevity Annuities are starting to
become popular for Income Later planning because
they have such a simple, transparent, and easy-to-
understand structure. A DIA is a pure pension plan
that efficiently solves for "longevity risk." More
carriers are starting to offer DIAs because consumers are demanding better lifetime income solutions
and benefits; they also want an option other than
Income Riders attached to deferred annuities.

Examples of Longevity Annuities (DIAs) are posted at The
AnnuityMan Steakhouse™ on my website, where you can request a proposal to fit your circumstances.

Long-Term Care Annuities

Long-Term Care (LTC) annuities are, in essence, a fixed annuity structure with long-term care or confinement care coverage
attached. Some are Fixed Annuities, and some are Fixed Index
Annuities (FIAs), either with the care benefit built in or attached
with a rider. LTC Annuities can be either guaranteed issue or
simplified issue—that is, set up by telephone interview and
without having to take a physical.

It's important to distinguish between Long-Term Care and
what's called Confinement Care. Long-Term Care annuities in

which you have to go through a simplified underwriting process are actually classified as health products, so they provide the same type of tax benefits as a traditional long-term care product. In contrast, with the kind of guaranteed issue coverage that includes an income rider attached to a deferred variable or indexed annuity, we normally classify that care benefit instead as Confinement Care, which provides no tax benefits when accessed. All money coming out of a guaranteed issue product is taxed at ordinary income tax levels.

Upside: LTC annuities allow you to retain full control of your money while retaining some long-term care coverage you might need. Usually a single premium product, LTC annuities avoid the possibility of rising premiums associated with traditional long-term care products. Also, if you never use the long-term care coverage, you still have a fixed annuity, 100 percent control of your money, and access to the lump sum. The guaranteed issue annuities in this category allow coverage for anyone who applies and can be a good supplemental coverage strategy.

Downside: LTC annuities have limited coverage in most cases and have age limitations for ownership. Also, fewer and fewer carriers are offering these products due to the new national healthcare plan that is now law. LTC annuities should only be used as a supplement to traditional long-term care, and never as a full replacement of that product.

Stanalysis©: If you have traditional long-term care, I would advise keeping your current policy because that is still the best coverage available.

Traditional LTC definitely has its place from a transfer of risk standpoint, and you might consider adding a LTC Annuity as additional coverage. If you can't qualify for the underwriting of traditional long-term care, then a LTC annuity, whether simplified or guaranteed issue, is a good alternative for this type of needed coverage despite its coverage limitations.

As always, The AnnuityMan Steakhouse™ at my website offers examples and opportunities to request proposals.

Multiple Benefit "Hybrid" Annuities (or "Unicorns")

The term "multiple benefit 'hybrid'" refers to annuities that provide multiple contractual benefits within one policy. The industry—particularly annuity wholesalers working directly with agents—have been using the word "hybrid" for over twenty years. However, just in the last few years, Internet annuity promoters have been overhyping the trendy word "hybrid" as the latest in a long list of useless sizzle words to entice you into buying an annuity. My running joke with the industry is that instead of "hybrid" why not use the word "unicorn" instead? People love unicorns! The bottom line is that when you hear the word "hybrid," it means that the annuity has more than one benefit within its structure. Want to know a dirty little secret?: *all* annuities have multiple benefits! Essentially, they all could be classified as "hybrid."

Here's a simple, easy-to-remember annuity formula:
Hybrid = Multiple Benefits.

Upside: With multiple benefit annuities you can package some benefits together under one contract using different riders. Typical offerings could include benefits like principal protection, long-term care/confinement care coverage, a guaranteed death benefit, lifetime income guarantees, and inflation adjustments.

Downside: When an annuity has multiple benefits within one contract structure, you typically see those multiple contractual guarantees at much lower levels than you would if you purchased one annuity to solve for one specific goal.

Stanalysis©: Hybrid is a car. Hybrid is a plant. Hybrid is not an annuity. If it sounds too good to be true, then it is...no exceptions. The annuity industry loves to package multiple benefit annuities as a one-stop shop to supposedly meet all of your needs. "Have your cake and eat it too" is a common and subtle annuity sales undertone. With any annuity purchase, you need to spell out exactly what you want the product to solve for, then seek the best contractual guarantee to solve for that one goal. In most cases, given that criterion of the highest contractual guarantee, you will not find what you are looking for in the overhyped "hybrid" annuity.

Traditional Fixed Annuity

A Traditional Fixed Annuity provides an interest rate that is guaranteed one year at a time. It will have an ongoing minimum guaranteed rate as well. A lot of times this strategy has some sort of up-front bonus to enhance the first-year return number, and it also allows you to add money to the policy at any time.

>**Upside:** Traditional Fixed Annuities normally track rising or falling interest rates, which can be a positive when it is time to renew or lock in the annual rate on your annuity anniversary date. They offer a good strategy to anyone looking not only to guarantee a fixed rate every year but to have a good chance of locking in any upswing in rates as well. Also, when compared to a Fixed Index Annuity (FIA), Traditional Fixed Annuities typically have a higher contractual minimum guarantee. Another plus is that few other fixed rate strategies allow you to add money to the policy after the contract has been issued and still benefit from the contractually guaranteed rate.

>**Downside:** When interest rates are low, Traditional Fixed Annuities are not very attractive. Many carriers stop offering them during those low rate periods. However, as rates move up, you will see this strategy come back into favor.

>**Stanalysis©:** For the person looking for fixed rate guarantees, a Traditional Fixed Annuity is a good strategy to lock in a rate annually and benefit from rising interest rates. I really like these products as a

unique and flexible addition to any fixed allocation part of a portfolio. I offer an example of a Traditional Fixed Annuity at The AnnuityMan Steakhouse™ on my website. I update and list these products on a monthly basis or whenever rates change.

Guaranteed Investment Contracts

Guaranteed Investment Contracts (GICs), also known as Guaranteed Interest Contracts, originated in the mid to late 1970s. A GIC is an insurance contract where the principal is guaranteed and the policyholder receives either a fixed or floating interest rate for a predetermined period of time. GICs are typically sold to institutions that qualify for favorable tax status, and they usually provide a higher guaranteed return than can be purchased with similar consumer products. The guaranteed period usually ranges from one to fifteen years.

A shorter term version of a GIC called a "Bullet GIC" is designed to take a single deposit—usually $100,000 or more—and provide a guaranteed annual interest rate for between three and seven years. Bullet GICs are primarily used in defined benefit plans in coordination with their scheduled plan contributions.

Upside: An institution, company, or ultra-high net worth investor will find that GICs can provide a higher guaranteed fixed rate than what "the street" offers. Usually negotiated with and created by the insurance carrier, GICs are typically customized for each specific situation.

Downside: GICs are very hard to find; most insurance carriers don't offer them anymore. Like all long-term fixed rate strategies, GICs are vulnerable to inflation. In addition, GICs are not guaranteed by any government body but are only backed by the issuing annuity carrier.

Stanalysis©: There's really no need for individuals to do much homework or shopping here. GICs might be available to you within your defined contribution plan, like a 401(k), so at least now you know what they are. GICs might also be offered within a salary reduction retirement plan sponsored by your employer. GICs will most likely become popular again once interest rates start to eventually rise.

Contingent Deferred Annuities

Relatively new to the financial world, but with the potential to be the "silicon valley" of the annuity industry, Contingent Deferred Annuities (CDAs) will grow quickly once consumers find out that you can own annuity–like guarantees without having to own an actual annuity. CDAs provide longevity risk protection, industry-speak for "not outliving your money." In essence, a CDA is a stand-alone guaranteed living withdrawal benefit you can attach to a nonannuity investment account.

Upside: The major benefit of a CDA is that when you attach it to a stock and bond portfolio you can achieve future lifetime income guarantees even when your investment account goes majorly south. There are no surrender charges, and you only pay an ongoing fee as long as it is "attached" to your investment account. Your portfolio is fully controlled by you, and the CDA just provides an income benefit layered on top of your investment account. The CDA will provide a lifetime income floor but allows you to still chase the dream of market returns.

Downside: Currently, only a handful of companies offer CDAs. Also, some of the better CDA offerings have limitations on which asset types and strategies your investment account can have. In other words, you cannot have your choice of any type of investment mix within the portfolio and simply attach a CDA contractual income benefit to the account. For now, to do so you have to follow certain portfolio rules.

Stanalysis©: If just the word "annuity" makes you want to vomit, but you still want contractual income guarantees, then this is your strategy. A CDA is an income rider without the annuity surrender charge commitment. With every major stock market correction, you will see this product category grow, because no matter how much people want guarantees, they will always yearn and dream for as much investment upside as possible.

Secondary Market Annuities

Secondary Market Annuities (SMAs) are a unique niche within the annuity world. Also known by their more clinical names; factored structured settlements, lottery winnings and immediate annuity reassignments, SMAs are owned by someone else who is now selling the guaranteed right to receive the contractual payments at a discounted purchase price in the secondary market. However, selling your annuity is not like selling your car. You actually have to receive a judge's approval (court order) under 26 USC § 5891 of the internal revenue code to change the payment rights of the policy, not to mention the issuing insurance company needs to acknowledge and approve the change—a process that can take a while. The taxation issues attached must be professionally handled by your CPA or tax lawyer. Only a handful of companies truly compete in this space, so the inventory of SMAs from which to choose is limited for now. However, with billions of annuities sold every year and trillions already on the books, SMA offerings will grow, and these strategies will become more popular.

> **Upside:** SMAs usually offer higher rates or higher payouts than primary market annuities. Large institutions, hedge funds, private equity firms, endowments, and high net worth individuals all use SMAs to achieve higher yields and to boost diversification within the fixed part of their portfolios.

> **Downside:** You need to have a true specialist in this area to handle any SMA transaction for you. Buying an SMA is not like buying a primary market annuity from your local agent; it requires patience and financial maturity. At a minimum, your CPA

should be involved, and I recommend consulting your lawyer as well. A very small subsection of the annuity world, SMA inventory is limited and available on a first-come, first-serve basis.

Stanalysis©: Even though I specialize only in annuities, I refer all of my SMA business to a good friend who only works in the secondary market world. He has lawyers and CPAs on staff to professionally handle every step of this process. If you have an interest in SMAs, contact me, and I will provide the needed introduction.

Specific Ways to Use Annuities

ANNUITIES FOR GROWTH

Let me go on record right here and say that in my opinion, annuities should not be considered as pure growth products. I know that puts me in the minority of agents who primarily sell variable and indexed products for potential market returns. However, as you know if you have read thus far, I feel strongly that annuities should only be owned for what they *will do*, not for what they *might do*. What does that mean in practical terms? It means that you should base any annuity buying decision solely on the contractual guarantees.

That said, pure tax-deferred growth can be achieved with a no-load variable annuity. I recommend no-load—that is, no fee—variable annuities because the average fees of a "loaded" variable annuity are over 3 percent annually and for the life of the policy. Also, whenever you purchase a loaded variable annuity and attach any rider for additional benefits to the policy, your carrier usually limits your internal investment choices from a contractual basis in order to lessen its risk.

No-load variable annuities are the best annuity structures available if tax-deferred growth is the goal. Agents cannot sell no-load products, so you will have to buy them direct.

ANNUITIES FOR INFLATION

Inflation is going to be "the gorilla in the room" for the foreseeable future. Few annuities really address inflation, and all of the carriers are hurrying to develop products to contractually combat this issue.

COLAs
Single Premium Immediate Annuities (SPIAs) and Longevity Annuities (DIAs) can combat inflation by attaching to the annuity policy a COLA (Cost of Living Adjustment) Rider that contractually increases your income stream by an annual percentage for as long as you live. For example, if you attach a 3 percent COLA Rider to a SPIA policy, the income stream derived from the initial premium will contractually increase by 3 percent annually for the rest of your life. You can choose any percentage increase at the time you fill out your annuity application, and that number cannot be changed.

Most people choose between 2 percent and 5 percent. Typically, 10 percent is the highest annual income stream increase that some annuity companies will contractually guarantee. Remember that when you attach any contractual increase to an annuity, the initial payout will be lower than that of the same annuity without one. I have examples of how COLA increases work on both SPIAs and DIAs at The AnnuityMan Steakhouse™ at my website

CPI-U

A few Fixed Index Annuities (FIAs) and SPIAs combat inflation by offering attached riders that will increase your income for life by following along with any CPI-U (Consumer Price Index for all Urban Consumers) increase. Some annuities offer income increases that lock in with any index option increase, and some will increase anytime CPI-U goes up, just like with Social Security payments. Go to The AnnuityMan Steakhouse™ at my website to see examples of how CPI-U increases work with annuities and to request a proposal.

Annual Ratchet or Lock In

Some fixed index annuities (FIAs) provide an income rider feature that you can contractually attach to your policy that will annually increase your lifetime payout by whatever growth percentage is achieved with the index option strategy. Before you get too excited about this, put your return expectations in line with reality when it comes to indexed annuities. These products were designed to compete with CDs, not the stock market, from a return standpoint. Your annual return—or "ratchet"—should realistically be around 1 percent to 4 percent.

This potential increase can be from the index option growth, a fixed rate amount, or a combination of both. However, the index option growth amounts are not guaranteed numbers; you are only guaranteed not to lose money if the index option expires worthless. If the index option does not create a positive return, you will receive no increase to your income for that year. These are good products—but not "too good to be true!" I further describe how an Annual Ratchet Strategy works at The AnnuityMan Steakhouse™ section of my website.

Hyperinflation

No annuity product on the planet will combat hyperinflation. It's really just that simple, so do not believe any hyperinflation annuity hype or projected number scenarios. Some ratchet products have annual caps on the income growth as high as 10 percent (attached to an index option), but those products still do not truly address hyperinflation in my opinion and are not that fluid of a strategy.

Advanced AnnuityMan™ Strategies

Regardless of what you are trying to solve for, annuities should only be owned for their contractual guarantees—the *only* thing you should consider when deciding to purchase an annuity. All of the strategies and numbers that I show are just the contractual guarantees, or worst-case scenario, a practice that sets Stan The Annuity Man® apart from everyone else in the annuity world. I keep screaming from the mountaintops that you own an annuity for what it *will do*, not what it *might do.* It is just that simple.

Every annuity plan that I put together for my clients is a customized solution based on their individual situation and date of birth. Over the years, I have developed unique, trademarked, and copyrighted solutions that might fit your needs and goals. Because annuity quotes and rates are constantly changing, I decided to open The AnnuityMan Steakhouse™ at my website in order to provide examples of the majority of annuity strategies I currently use. Why a steakhouse you ask? Because you should buy an annuity for the *steak,* not the sizzle. Every month, the numbers will be updated to reflect current rates and product offerings, so I suggest you plan on visiting The AnnuityMan Steakhouse™ every month just to keep up with the ever-changing menu!

The product descriptions, applications, and strategies in this book and displayed at The AnnuityMan Steakhouse™ offer insight to how I use annuities to contractually solve problems. By no means is every strategy I use or have developed included. However, your glimpse into the world of Stan The Annuity Man's unique and customized recommendations should also help you decide if a contractually guaranteed annuity strategy is right for your own situation.

Before we get to the actual strategies, it is important to build the foundation on how and why these annuity strategies work.

Fixed Annuities *Only*

Stan The Annuity Man currently uses only fixed annuities with my customized strategies. The main problem with variable annuities is the word "variable." You know my saying—and future tattoo, if my wife allows it: "Own an annuity for what it *will do,* not what it *might do.*" Variable annuities are one big "might do" and the primary reason all my strategies involve fixed annuities. I live in Annuity Realityville, not Annuity Dreamworld.

I use fixed annuities exclusively because they are 100 percent principal protected and because the fees are substantially lower than variable annuities. More importantly, the actuarial payout percentages are consistently higher. I run *all* of my proposals and recommendations at the contractually guaranteed level the policy offers. In other words, I will show you the worst-case scenario to help you make your decision only on the contractual certainties—a practice that separates Stan The Annuity Man from most everyone else out there recommending annuities. I do not sell dreams, I sell contractual guaranteed realities.

Transfer of Risk

Transfer of risk is the cornerstone of any Stan The Annuity Man strategy. Annuity companies, in essence, will shoulder the risk of the goal or problem that you want them to solve. For example, when you buy a lifetime income annuity, the insurance company will pay you for the rest of your life regardless of how long you live. They are accepting the risk of you living a very long time and past your life expectancy, which will ensure that you will never outlive your money (what we call "longevity risk").

The AnnuityMan™ Strategies: Leveraging, Laddering, Splitting

When you call yourself Stan The Annuity Man, you are an admitted quant when it comes to annuities. Because my father was a phenomenal math mind, math major, and math teacher after his coaching days ended, I was taught at an early age that numbers matter. Numbers should not lie. That is the way I look at annuities. I consider them only as mathematical contractual guarantees. The annuity policy will tell you exactly how the product works and what it will do.

With that common sense and realistic approach—along with the fact that I am independent and can represent almost every annuity company out there—my staff and I are constantly looking for ways to maximize annuity guarantees. Over the years, I have developed numerous leveraging, laddering, arbitrage, and combination strategies which have left the carriers and the annuity industry scratching their heads at my quant approach; meanwhile, my clients continue to take advantage of the contractual guarantees in place. Below are just a few of the large inventory of ideas I have created. Please understand that all annuity strategies are customizable, so let me know what you are trying to achieve, and we might develop and name a strategy after you!

Leveraging Annuities

I am constantly looking at the contractual guarantees of all kinds of annuities, sometimes using those guarantees in leveraged combinations to achieve a client's specific goals. I have developed unique and proprietary leveraged strategies for both income and legacy planning.

Leveraged Income Doubler©

The first leveraged strategy I developed, Leveraged Income Doubler© (LID), began as the impetus for me to be constantly searching for contractually leveraged opportunities using multiple carriers. The LID strategy involves using a Fixed Indexed Annuity (FIA) combined with Flexible Premium Annuity, which work together to provide the maximum contractual income possible. The AnnuityMan Steakhouse™ on my website displays an example of the LID strategy and the opportunity to request a specific LID proposal for your situation.

Annuity Arbitrage

The Annuity Arbitrage strategy leverages annuities and life insurance at the same time to achieve contractually guaranteed goals for legacy and lifetime income. The strategy involves using part or all of the income stream from a SPIA to purchase a life insurance policy. What you achieve is a lifetime income stream, normally set up jointly with your spouse, and a lump sum tax-free death benefit as well. Most of my advanced strategies will involve your estate planning lawyer and CPA, with this particular Annuity Arbitrage plan sometimes involving an Irrevocable Life Insurance Trust as part of the structure. To see a specific example of the Annuity Arbitrage strategy and to request a proposal, go to The AnnuityMan Steakhouse™ at my website.

IRA Ray Mirror™

Another legacy strategy of mine actually was suggested by a good friend and client who also happens to be one of the leading insurance consultants and actuaries in the country. Named the IRA Ray Mirror™ strategy, its conception hit both of us in an "aha moment" as we were discussing how to leverage contractual death benefits offered within an individual annuity policy. Yes, I consider those types of conversations fun! Hey, I'm Stan The Annuity Man! And the client's name, as you probably have guessed, is Ray.

The IRA Ray Mirror™ strategy involves using the same annuity in an IRA and also in a non-IRA account with the same dollar amount invested in each. That multiple dollar requirement alone limits most from implementing, but for those who qualify, this is a no-brainer. It is a little complicated, but the strategy revolves around taking your RMDs out of your IRA and using both policies in conjunction to contractually guarantee that you will end up with more total money than you started with. It works regardless of how long you live and how many RMDs you take. To see an example of the IRA Ray Mirror™ strategy, as always go to The AnnuityMan Steakhouse™ at my website.

Laddering Annuities

Most investors are familiar with laddering CDs or laddering bonds—a timeless strategy that makes complete common sense for people who are trying not to "time" interest rate movements. The same laddering strategy can be done with annuities. I sometimes call it "stacking income."

Lifetime Ladder™

I have developed a strategy called Lifetime Ladder™ to combat low interest rate environments. One way to do this is to buy a SPIA on an annual basis to take advantage of the higher payouts you will receive because you are older and have a shorter life expectancy. Furthermore, you hope for rising interest rates as well. A few other ways to ladder annuities is to use Fixed Rate Annuities, just like you would with CDs or bonds, and also using multiple Income Later contractual guarantees with lifetime income streams starting at different intervals. Examples of Lifetime Ladder™ strategies are at The AnnuityMan Steakhouse™ section of my website.

Split Annuity Combinations (Annuity Buckets)

The Split Annuity Combination strategy has been around the annuity industry for decades, but it is seldom used or even fully understood by most agents. Split Annuity Strategies— also known as Annuity Buckets or income buckets—are not one-size-fits-all, and I have used as few as two and as many as seven annuities simultaneously to contractually achieve a customized client goal. The AnnuityMan Steakhouse™ on my website lists specific examples of Split Annuity Combination strategies and, as always, you can request a proposal that fits your needs.

Is My Money Safe with an Annuity?

The Annuity Company Itself
(the Issuer)

The first line of defense, and the first place that you have to depend on for the safety of your money, is the company that issued the annuity policy to you. Annuity guarantees are only as good as the company standing behind those promises. I highly recommend going to a company's website and researching its strength and safety. Also, ask your agent and advisor for any additional industry information that he or she can provide so that you can do the proper due diligence before purchasing an annuity from that company.

Insurance Company Ratings

As with stocks and bonds, insurance companies that issue annuities are rated for safety as well. A.M. Best is probably the most widely recognized resource for annuity carrier ratings.

Standard and Poor's, Fitch, Moody's, and Weiss also provide financial ratings and analyze the risk of insurance companies. In my opinion, none of these services are better than the other, and all should be used when considering an annuity purchase.

COMDEX™ RANKINGS

One of the primary tools I use to evaluate companies for client recommendations is the COMDEX™, a composite index insurance company score based on the ratings received from multiple rating agencies. It is easy for most people to understand because a perfect score is 100. The score is expressed by the average percentile ranking for all of the ratings and is a pretty good objective scale to compare different companies. What I like about it most is that the COMDEX™ score is a valuation that bases its calculations on ratings from A.M. Best, Standard and Poor's, Moody's Investors Service, and Fitch. That is why Stan The Annuity Man exclusively uses COMDEX™ as my primary source for looking at a company's ratings stability. Instead of the nebulous letter ratings of A, B, AA, and so on that none of us really understand, COMDEX™ scores from 1 to 100 just makes common sense.

If you would like to see a full listing of current COMDEX™ rankings, I offer a complimentary PDF download that's updated monthly under the "Resources" tab of my website. Use it to aid in your carrier due diligence. The full COMDEX™ report, usually around 20 pages, includes the COMDEX™ score for each annuity carrier along with the individual ratings of the four major ratings agencies.

NOLHGA: State Guaranty Funds

Annuities are regulated at the state level, not at the federal level as securities are. Each state has a specific guaranty fund that backs all annuities issued in that state up to a specific dollar limit. To find out the coverage for your state go to www.nolhga.com. NOLHGA stands for the National Organization of Life and Health Insurance Guaranty Associations. If something goes wrong with the carrier, NOLHGA is the next level of protection for your money.

By the way, an agent or advisor cannot describe the state guaranty fund as resembling FDIC coverage because it is not! The state guaranty funds cannot be used in sales materials or as the primary basis for any annuity recommendation. The NOLHGA is not FDIC insurance like you have at your bank account, period. Both provide limited coverage but are completely different animals—similar in function but definitely *not* the same.

If you become a Stan The Annuity Man® client, I will fully explain how your state coverage applies to your individual annuity strategy in case you are worried about having multiple layers of protection for your money.

The Annuity Industry "Conglomerate"

It is my opinion that at the end of the day annuities are "confidence" products...period. And believe me, the annuity and life insurance industry not only knows this but definitely wants to protect this ongoing "confidence" with both current and future clients. In other words, the industry pretty much self-regulates in order to keep this ongoing consumer "confidence" in place and to keep the money flowing in. The bottom line is that when compared to other strategies for your money, annuities are a comparably safe place for at least a portion of your portfolio.

When you decide to purchase an annuity, your carrier shoulders the risk that you have decided to transfer to it. If you purchased a lifetime income annuity, then you expect that annuity company to pay you for your life…regardless of how long you live. You have confidence that the annuity company is going to pay you for life, and the entire annuity industry knows that…and takes that promise very seriously. The industry will do whatever it takes to protect the annuity golden goose.

What Is Guaranteed within the Annuity Contract?

Guaranteed Minimum Value

The Guaranteed Minimum is the worst-case scenario "walk-away" amount offered in most deferred annuities available today. With Fixed Rate Annuities (MYGAs), Fixed Indexed Annuities (FIAs), Traditional Fixed Annuities, and Flexible Premium Fixed Annuities, you are guaranteed to receive a minimum percentage annually and get back more money at the end of the contract than your initial deposit amount if no money is withdrawn from the policy.

Death Benefit and Legacy Benefits

Some annuities can attach a rider, or additional benefit, to a policy to guarantee some percentage growth amount that you can leave to your listed beneficiaries. Such death benefits are separate, worst-case scenario calculations within your annuity contract. If the accumulation value (investment side) is higher than the guaranteed death benefit calculation, then your beneficiaries will receive the higher of the two calculations as the death benefit. The contractual death benefit rider serves as a guaranteed "floor" amount for legacy and estate planning purposes. Most annuity death benefit riders pay out that death benefit over a five-year time period to your listed beneficiaries.

It is important to remember that with annuities the death benefit does not pass tax-free to your beneficiaries the way traditional life insurance does. Annuities do avoid probate issues, just like life insurance, but the annuity asset will be included as part of your estate from a tax standpoint. To see specific examples of how contractual death benefits with annuities work, go to The AnnuityMan Steakhouse™ at my website and request a proposal.

Lifetime Income Benefits (also known as Living Benefits)

Income riders can be added to some annuity contracts to provide a contractually guaranteed annual growth percentage that can be used in the future for lifetime income payments. Income riders should be attached to Fixed Annuities or FIAs but not variable annuities because the customer typically does better from a cost and actuarial percent payout standpoint. Your lifetime income stream calculation will be based on whichever is higher at the time you decide to start taking income, the accumulation value or the guaranteed income rider calculation.

The contractual Lifetime Income Benefits serve as a guaranteed "floor" so that when you do Target Date or Income Later income planning you will know to the penny what your lifetime payout will be.

Long-Term Care/Confinement Care Benefits

Some annuities offer Riders (similar to income riders) that will cover future long-term care/confinement care type payments. Some Long-Term Care Riders will double your income stream if LTC coverage is needed and if you qualify for this enhanced benefit based on the specific annuity contract. Other LTC riders will offer some form of increasing payment if you need confinement care coverage. All of these LTC riders are different, so it is important to understand the specific contractual rules to determine which one is best for you.

Qualification for LTC coverage is usually triggered when you cannot perform two of the six activities of daily living, which are eating, bathing, dressing, toileting, transferring (walking), and continence. Current studies show that when you cannot perform two of these six activities, you will live an average of three years and a maximum of seven years. Insurance companies base their actuarial calculations and benefits offered on a combination of these types of long-term care studies along with your specific life expectancy.

Go to The AnnuityMan Steakhouse™ at my website to see specific examples of these LTC/Confinement Care riders, and to request a specific proposal for your situation.

Creditors and Lawsuits

In some states, for example, Florida and Texas, annuities can provide protection from creditors and predatory or frivolous lawsuits when policies are structured properly. However, like everything in life, it is not that simple. These statutes have been challenged in court over the years. For example, if you know that you are close to going bankrupt or know that you are getting ready to be sued, you just cannot buy a bunch of annuities to protect the money. You have to be able to show that the annuities were in place way before any potential problems were about to arise.

However, when used correctly and as a preemptive measure, annuities and life insurance can provide solid protection from "predators." My advice is to consult with your qualified CPA and lawyers concerning this type of annuity protection before implementing any asset protection strategies. I will work with your team to put together a customized plan to achieve your asset protection goals.

Essential Annuity Specifics

How Gains Are Credited to a Fixed Annuity

The first thing that happens when you buy an annuity is that you pay the insurance company a premium, that is, the initial money. Next, the insurance company puts the majority of that money into reserve, pays expenses—including the agent's commission—and invests the remainder. These investments are usually in some type of fixed-rate bond that matches the surrender period of the policy you own. When you initially purchase an annuity, the insurance company actually *loses* money. That is why there are surrender penalties to recapture those losses if you cash out of a deferred annuity.

For example, let's assume the bond in which the insurance company invests your premium earns 5 percent annually. The insurance company will take 2 percent to maintain your policy, and also for profit. The remaining 3 percent is either credited to your account (in the case of MYGAs or Traditional Fixed Annuities) or is used to purchase a call option with specific terms (in the case of FIAs, or Indexed Annuities).

The only difference as far as the insurance company is concerned between giving you the 3 percent or using the 3 percent to buy an option is the timing of when they credit any potential interest to your account. Traditional Fixed Annuities and MYGAs get credited throughout the year; FIAs (indexed annuities) get credited at the end of the contract anniversary each year, and after the outcome of the option is known.

What Is a Rider?

A rider is an attached benefit that can be added to a Deferred Annuity or Immediate Annuity contract. For Immediate Annuities, the typical rider that you can attach is a COLA, or Cost of Living Adjustment. For Deferred Annuities, there are Death Benefit Riders that provides contractual guarantees for legacy, and there are income riders that provide contractual guarantees of future lifetime income. There are even Long Term Care/Confinement Care riders that provide a transfer of risk for this type of coverage. Most income riders cannot be issued to someone less than forty years old or, in most cases, older than eighty.

The key point to remember about any annuity rider is that it is *not* a walk-away amount. You can *never* get the money out in a lump sum while you are alive! This is why income riders are sometimes referred to as "living benefits."

I wish the annuity industry would rename this benefit, because as we all know, no one "rides" for free! A rider is a specific contractual benefit that is attached to your annuity contract. For example, you can attach an income rider to provide for lifetime income. You can attach a death benefit rider to guarantee a specific death benefit. The long-term care/confinement riders described above can transfer the risk for that type of coverage. Please understand that your rider calculation is totally separate from your other annuity contract calculations, such as Accumulation Value, Surrender Value, and Minimum Guarantee Value.

Rider valuations can only be used for the specific benefit each mentions. For example, an income rider that grows by 6 percent annually during the time you are waiting to turn on the income stream can *only* be used for income. Again, you cannot access that money in a lump sum. That is where the industry is having some problems based on how it presents the product. Whether the industry intends it or not, many people believe they own an annuity yielding 6 percent like the old CDs they remember from the Jimmy Carter years.

The truth is that they own a 6 percent income rider that can only be used for income. That's OK if the goal is Target Date or Income Later planning. Sadly, I receive calls every day in which people are confused about how their riders (attached benefits) actually work within their annuity contract. Know what you are buying, and know what you own. And more important, as I have written before: if it sounds too good to be true, then it is. No exceptions.

Up-front Bonuses

Some Deferred Annuities offer an up-front bonus percentage that will be added to your contract on day one. For example, if a Deferred Annuity has a 6 percent up-front bonus and you place $100,000 into the contract, your initial balance will be $106,000

($100,000 + $6,000). Too many of these up-front bonuses are also improperly sold, and most agents and advisors overemphasize them. It's also important to point out that most of these bonuses fall under a vesting schedule as well.

You should not base your decision to buy an annuity on a bonus, and you should never transfer your current annuity with surrender charges because you were told that the bonus will "make up for it." Transferring annuities should be about upgrading your annuity, not making a bonus possibly cover or offset a surrender charge. I always tell people that buying an annuity for the bonus is like buying a car for the stereo. It makes no sense!

Internal Fees and Surrender Charges

Take both fees and surrender charges into consideration when purchasing the appropriate annuity solution. Most fixed annuities (SPIAs, DIAs, MYGAs, FIAs, Traditional Fixed, Flexible Fixed, and so on) have no internal fees unless a rider is attached to the policy. Other annuities (like VAs) have annual internal fees associated with the product; these should be understood in detail before purchasing.

It is very important to remember that, with a few exceptions, Deferred Annuities have surrender charges during the specified contract period. For example, a ten-year Deferred Annuity will have declining surrender charges over that ten-year time period. Always have your agent or advisor fully explain all of the internal fees and surrender charges before you add any annuity to your portfolio.

Annuity Policy Values

Your annuity statement will display different policy values. Most likely, they will all be different dollar valuations. It's important to know what each line items means to fully understand your annuity policy. Let's compare the different valuations you may encounter.

Accumulation Value

I really wish that the annuity industry would re-name Accumulation Value to Real Money Value. The Accumulation Value is simply your premium plus interest (bonus, index credits, interest rate, mutual fund returns, and so on). It is the value you can walk away with after the surrender period is over, and it is the value that surrender charges are assessed against.

In recent years, the explanation of the Accumulation Value has been "blurred" in my opinion. When you own an annuity with an income rider—again, an attached benefit—that is a separate, stand-alone calculation distinct from the Accumulation Value. Your income rider value will never be a "walk-away" amount or accessible in a lump sum.

Surrender Value

All Deferred Annuities have surrender charges if you get out of the annuity contract early. If you bought a five-year CD and decided to fully cash out in year two, you would be charged a surrender penalty of a specified percentage to get your money out; Deferred Annuities work the same way. Most Deferred Annuity surrender charges decline over time.

For example, a five-year annuity might have surrender charges of 6 percent in year one, 5 percent in year two, 4 percent in year three, 3 percent in year four, and 2 percent in the final year of the policy. Most Deferred Annuities allow you to withdraw 10 percent of the Accumulation Value on an annual basis without a surrender charge. Single Premium Immediate Annuities, Longevity Annuities, and Charitable Gift Annuities do not have surrender charges because there is usually no liquidity to those types of income contracts. All Deferred Annuities base their surrender charges on the specified term in the contract.

Lifetime Income Value

If you have attached an income rider to your annuity policy, this value is a separate and stand-alone calculation that describes the value to be used at the time you decide to turn on the lifetime income stream.

Income riders usually provide a guaranteed percentage growth amount as long as you are deferring, and this income value can only be used for lifetime income. You cannot access this value in a lump sum or transfer it to another annuity. In addition, if the income value is not used, it disappears upon the death of the annuity owner with most policies.

Death Benefit Value

Similar to an income rider, a Death Benefit Rider is designed to guarantee a growth amount that can be used for legacy. Obviously, a death benefit value can only be distributed upon the death of the annuity policy owner. Most contractual Death Benefit Riders attached to Deferred Annuities are paid out over a five-year time period to the listed beneficiaries. Also, if the Accumulation Value—that is, the "walk-away"—is higher than the contractual death benefit, then the owner's beneficiaries will receive the higher of the two valuations.

Market Value-Adjustment Value

The market value-adjustment valuation (MVA), primarily used with indexed annuities, will adjust the value of your annuity whenever a withdrawal is subject to a surrender charge. MVAs on variable annuities are simply calculated on the separate account (also known as mutual funds) valuations.

Here's all you need to know about MVAs. If interest rates go up after you have purchased your annuity, then your MVA is negative and your surrender charges would increase. If interest rates go down after you have purchased your annuity, then your MVA is positive and your surrender charges would decrease as well. In some cases when interest rates really go south after you bought the annuity, your surrender charges might even disappear from a valuation standpoint.

Minimum Guarantee Value

Most deferred annuity contracts have a minimum guarantee value. This is a separate calculation that you should view as a worst-case scenario "walk-away" amount.

Actuarial Percentage Payout

The actuarial percentage payout is the most important part of any annuity lifetime income calculation. The actuarial payout is the specific percentage that the annuity company assigns to your lifetime income stream at the time you elect to start the income. For example, if you have a $100,000 Single Premium Immediate Annuity and your actuarial percentage payout is 7 percent at the time you turn on the lifetime income stream, then your lifetime annual income payout is $7,000 (0.07 × $100,000 = $7,000).

Your actuarial percentage payout, primarily based on your life expectancy, determines how all income streams are derived from annuities. However, among annuity companies no real uniformity of actuarial payout exists, regardless of your age. It will vary from company to company and product to product. For this reason, it is so important to shop numerous carriers for the best contractual guaranteed payout.

A captive agent who only represents one company or a handful of them is like a paint store that only sells a few colors. You need to use the services of a true independent agent, or multiple agents, and force them to show you as many carrier quotes as possible, in conjunction with reviewing their COMDEX™ rankings.

"Free Look" Period

Annuities are regulated at the state level. Each state has a "free look" period in place that allows you to fully review the contract after it has been delivered, giving you the opportunity to receive a full refund if you are not completely satisfied with the policy that you purchased. No questions are asked why, and you need give no reasons to get your money back in full.

Look up your state department of insurance to see what the "free look" period is for your state. In fact, your agent and advisor should inform you of the time period during the sales process but especially when the policy is delivered. The "free look" period starts from the time you sign and date a receipt affirming delivery of the annuity policy contract to you. The annuity policy is still contractually in force during the "free look" period even while you are reviewing the policy after delivery.

Transferring Annuities
(1035 Exchange and Direct Transfer)

If you currently own a Deferred Annuity, you can transfer it without tax implications to another annuity. Single Premium Immediate Annuities (SPIAs), Longevity Annuities (DIAs), and Charitable Gift Annuities (CGAs) cannot be transferred under the 1035 exchange rule.

If you decide to transfer your annuity to another annuity, the agent or advisor has to prove in writing during the application process that the transfer would be in your best interest and is a contractual upgrade from what you currently own. The main thing to remember is that transferring from one annuity to another annuity is a "nontaxable" event, regardless of whether the annuity is in an IRA or non-IRA account. Also, the cost basis from your old annuity will transfer to your new annuity.

You can transfer your current annuity without tax consequences in one of two ways. The first is via the IRS 1035 exchange rule for nonqualified (non-IRA) accounts; the second is by a direct transfer for qualified (IRA) accounts. If your annuity is housed within a non-IRA account, then you would use the 1035 "annuity to annuity" exchange rule. Otherwise, if your annuity is within your IRA, then you follow the direct "IRA to IRA" transfer rule. In both instances, the money is transferred from one financial institution or carrier directly to another financial institution or carrier. Again, these moves are nontaxable events.

Annuities and Taxes

Even though annuities are issued by life insurance companies, they do not have the same tax advantages as life insurance. Whereas life insurance proceeds pass tax-free to the listed beneficiaries of the policy, annuity death benefit proceeds do not.

Also, annuity income streams are taxed differently with Single Premium Immediate Annuities and Deferred Annuities, and differently when the money is in an IRA versus a non-IRA. Agents and advisors are *not* tax advisors and should not be filling that role for you in any capacity. Always work closely with your CPA and qualified tax advisors concerning any annuity tax question. For any type of estate planning involving annuities, I recommend consulting with an estate planning lawyer who is familiar with your state laws.

Types of Accounts
Annuities can be held in both IRA (qualified) and non-IRA (nonqualified) accounts. IRA accounts can be traditional IRAs as well as Roth IRAs. Qualified

accounts can also include other types of retirement plans.

Tax Deferral
Currently, annuities are one of the few financial vehicles that enjoy tax-free growth in deferral. Gains or interest credits are not taxed until they are taken out.

Ordinary Income
Any time you take money out of an annuity it is taxed as ordinary income.

LIFO
Last In First Out (LIFO) is the accounting method used for all nonqualified annuities purchased after 1982. LIFO means that the gains are taken out first and taxed first.

IRS Section 1035
If you are the type who loves to read manuals and know all of the details about the most mundane things, then IRS Section 1035 is the place to go to learn everything about annuities and their corre-sponding tax ramifications. Again, I want to empha-size the importance of always using a qualified tax advisor for any specific annuity tax question. Don't be a "do it yourselfer" when it comes to taxes, and certainly do not depend on an annuity agent for tax advice.

Exclusion Ratio

The exclusion ratio calculation is used when you "annuitize," or create a series of payments or a lifetime income stream. Annuitization is the combination of return of principal and interest, so the "exclusion ratio" applies to the principal part of the income stream payment. The principal is excluded from taxes. Exclusion ratios only apply to annuitization in a non-IRA (non-qualified) account. If you have an annuity within an IRA type account, there is no exclusion ratio.

Premium Tax

Some states, for example California and Nevada, have instituted a premium tax on income derived from annuities. The carriers are actually building in this tax within the contractually guaranteed quotes in order to lessen the shock, but the tax is there. Because annuities are regulated at the state level, and states seem to always need more revenue, I predict that more and more states will start implementing this type of annuity premium tax.

RMDs

Required Minimum Distributions (RMDs) have to occur with all IRAs when you turn 70 ½. If you have an annuity inside of your IRA, the RMD rule applies to that annuity asset as well.

The Rule of 72(t) & 72(q) / 59 ½ Penalty

Because annuity growth is tax-deferred, the government has special rules restricting when and how you can use the money in them. The basic rule is that if you are under 59 ½, you will pay a 10 percent penalty on any money you have not paid taxes on yet. For qualified money, this results in a 10 percent penalty on all funds taken out. For non-qualified, the penalty will be on the gains. A number of exceptions to this rule exist, such as hardship, disability, a first-time home purchase, and so on, but for most people this rule will apply.

Ways to avoid this penalty do exist and are covered by Sections 72(t) and 72(q) of the tax code. In simplified terms, these rules say that if you want to avoid the under 59 ½ penalty you must take the funds out in a systematic manner. That means the distribution will be based on your life expectancy, and taken out for a minimum of five years or to age 59 ½, whichever is *later*.

If you decide you want to implement a 72(t)-72(q) strategy, be sure to work with both a CPA and the insurance company that holds your annuity, because all carriers handle these rules differently from an administrative standpoint.

Agent Fees and Commissions

Annuities are life insurance products and issued by life insurance companies. All life insurance products and annuities offered by agents or advisors pay commissions to them. However, those commissions are "built in" to the product, so you will not see them listed on your annuity statement.

For example, if you buy an annuity with $100,000, you will see $100,000 go to work and on your statement. Rest assured that a commission or fee was paid to your agent or advisor. Do not allow agents to play semantic word games or let them get away with saying that they were not compensated, that no agent fee exists, or that they do not charge a fee. You know better than that.

A rule of thumb on commissions is that the longer the surrender charge period is, the higher the commission to the agent. A ten-year deferred indexed or variable annuity with ten years of surrender charges would pay a very high commission to the agent. A SPIA would pay a very low commission, as would a short-term (two to five years) Fixed Rate Annuity (MYGA).

The only annuity products that do not pay a commission are no-load annuities that you have to buy directly from the carrier. Most of the no-load annuities available are variable annuities, and ironically, those are the only variable annuities I currently like in that product category.

The AnnuityMan™ Professor

//

In the Stan The Annuity Man world of annuity strategies, the P.I.L.L.© acronym is an easy way to find out if you even need an annuity. If you do not need Principal Protection, Income for Life, Legacy, or Long Term Care type benefits, then you do not need an annuity. It is just that simple. I live in Annuity Realityville, where I never sell the dream of potential returns, only the contractually guaranteed realities.

That being said, it is worth noting that annuities are really contractual math products. It's all about the numbers and what the annuity policy guarantees in writing. The true actuarial quant types in the annuity world use calculations like IRR, ILY, Income Value, and Annuity Yield Curve to explain how the annuity engine really works. I hope my explanations will help you understand what all of the annuity academic fuss is about.

Internal Rate of Return

Normally, people use Internal Rate of Return (IRR) to evaluate the investment returns of CDs or bonds. With annuity IRR calculations for Single Premium Immediate Annuities and Deferred Income Annuities, we use a combination of both investment and insurance components—a method that is a bit different from most IRR calculations.

All Stan The Annuity Man® income annuity quotes can provide this IRR calculation based on your own situation upon request.

Implied Longevity Yield®

Moshe Milevsky, a leading thinker, researcher, and commentator in the field of finance and insurance developed and trademarked the Implied Longevity Yield® (ILY) calculation. What separates IRR from ILY is that to find IRR you have to know how many years annuity payments will be made. With ILY calculations, payments are made for the life of the annuitant, so we cannot know that number until the policy owner dies.

The longer you wait to start your lifetime income stream, the higher your payment will be, given that annuity income payments are based on your life expectancy. ILY calculates what yield you would have to achieve from a nonannuity product that would match the lifetime income stream guarantees of an income annuity. ILY can help you decide whether it would make sense to own an income annuity right now or wait until a later date.

All Stan The Annuity Man® income annuity quotes can provide this ILY calculation based on your situation upon request.

Income Value and Income Annuity Yield Curve

Once a contract is turned into income through annuitization, it no longer has an accumulation or surrender value. It is hard to track this asset on financial statements. This is especially true of lifetime income, because no one knows for sure how much income you are going to receive. Because of this, the industry has come up with a method of calculating the "value" of an asset that technically has no value beyond the income it provides. That number is called Income Value.

One piece of the Income Value calculation is the Income Annuity Yield Curve, a set of rates similar to the US Treasury curve. The difference is that this yield curve reflects the pricing and credit experience of the companies in the industry that provide guaranteed lifetime income products.

The Income Annuity Yield Curve, published on a daily basis, is available through Stan The Annuity Man® upon request. We can also show you a comparison of the Income Annuity Yield Curve with the US Treasury curve if you are really into that kind of stuff!

Life Expectancy

Without getting too technical, we can say that the primary factor that determines the amount of your income stream will be your life expectancy when you decide to start the annuity payments. As a good friend of mine in the life insurance business says, "One out of one of us will die." Pretty motivating, right? Just as we all know this statement to be brutally correct, annuity carriers must base their pricing on that reality, too.

In essence, when you buy an income annuity of any type, you are betting with the annuity company that you will live longer than they think you will live. And if you do live longer—regardless of how long that is—they will have to pay you. That is the elevator pitch and definition of solving for "longevity risk."

Return on Investment

When we look at Return on Investment (ROI), you will find that this is where Stan The Annuity Man departs from the position of most annuity agents. Here's why: I do not think annuities should be considered as growth products. Even though the vast majority of annuities sold annually are variable annuities with growth exposure via their separate accounts (that is, through mutual funds), I still stand firm on this annuity nongrowth issue. To me, true growth involves limitless investment choices and complete flexibility to achieve your desired return.

Even the best no-load variable annuity—among the over three hundred fund choices currently available—is still limited from a choice standpoint. In addition, an ugly little secret about fixed index annuities is that they were actually designed to compete with CD returns, not market returns. So those strategies are not worth addressing from a pure growth standpoint in my opinion.

Annuities should be considered only as "transfer of risk" strategies that solve for specific goals—primarily lifetime income. To start comparing annuities to other investments from an ROI standpoint is a waste of time. Like comparing apples to oranges.

Annuity Quotation Systems

Because I only focus on the contractual guarantees of any type of annuity, my staff and I have developed proprietary annuity quotation systems to filter hundreds of the top annuity company products and locate for you the best contractual solution available. CANNEX™, the primary company that we use, is the industry leader in providing the best contractually guaranteed annuity quotes for your specific situation, and we have worked closely with them for years.

AnnuityMan™ Views and Commentary

I never shy away from stating my opinion when it comes to annuities. I write numerous national columns that address annuities from both the consumer and industry standpoints. I encourage you to frequently visit my website for up to date commentary on the world of annuities. The "Resources" tab on my Stan The Annuity Man® website is the best place to go if you want to educate yourself about all things annuity.

Living in Annuityville
(also known as Annuity Realityville)

I get a ton of phone calls from people who have purchased an annuity but have no clue about what they actually own. Usually they spit out a few bullet points from the sales presentation, futilely hoping that the "sounds too good to be true" reasons they bought the annuity have a basis in reality. Too often, they do not.

Annuity Realityville is a place I never leave. I love living there. It is a place where we only consider the contractual guarantees, and we fully explain and understand the good and the bad of every strategy before we make any decisions. In our utopian Annuityville, we also have no urgency to buy any annuity; we implement any transfer of risk strategy only on the customer's time frame. Annuities are fantastic products when allocated properly within a portfolio. They are not "one size fits all" solutions, nor do they fit into the "better than sliced bread" trophy case.

My advice to everyone who feels pressured into buying annuity is to write down exactly how you understand the product works according to the sales presentation that you heard. After you list everything, then simply sign and date it. The next step is to turn the paper around, slide it to the annuity agent, and have him or her sign and date it as well. Run a copy of it for your records, then ask the agent to include the original within the annuity application package that is sent to the annuity company.

In other words, have that annuity agent fully stand behind his or her recommendation. If he or she will do so, then you are covered. However, you might find that the pen gets pretty heavy for that agent to pick up—especially if that presentation had too much sizzle and not enough steak! Do not take someone's sales presentation word for it. Get those words in writing.

How Interest Rates Affect Annuities

One of the primary pricing cornerstones for all annuity policies is the ten-year US Treasury rate, the benchmark rate to follow. Annuity income streams are priced using your actuarial life expectancy as well as current interest rates.

Common sense would tell you that if interest rates are higher, you would find better annuity pricing. That is a fact. The problem, as you know, is trying to predict where interest rates are going to go. No one knows—not me, not you, not most so-called interest rate experts! If your gut feel tells you that rates are low but might rise in the near future, then I would recommend possibly "laddering" your annuity purchases over time.

Politics and Annuities

With trillions of dollars of annuities already on the books and hundreds of billions being purchased every year, our friendly politicians have put a bull's-eye on annuities. They see a ripe, juicy fruit they want to squeeze the potential tax revenue out of. So far, the annuity lobbyists have kept these "tax and spenders" at bay, but it is only a matter of time until both Washington and the states themselves start targeting annuities as a rich and ongoing revenue source. Some states have already begun their "taxing creativity."

Premium Tax

Currently, a few states have imposed a "premium tax" on any income stream that originates from an annuity. Because all annuities are regulated at the state level, annuities are a logical taxing target. After all, baby boomer and retirees need annuity type income, and, oh, by the way, over ten thousand baby boomers retire every day. Our political friends are well aware of that statistic. Do not be surprised if somehow the federal government tries to get its share of the annuity tax pie as well by implementing a similar type of premium tax on annuity income.

State and Local Pensions

Some states are seeing a legislative push to possibly transfer the public pension responsibilities from the state to private insurance/annuity companies. Conceptually, I love less government, but I am not sure that this will ever happen legislatively or be approved by labor union leadership. This is another one of those good ideas that probably does not have the political legs to get implemented.

Annuity Trends
(Current and Future)

So with those ten thousand baby boomers who are retiring every day, we can expect the need for contractual guarantees and benefits to continue to grow. People want safety, and they want income that they cannot outlive. In the annuity industry, not outliving your money is called solving for "longevity risk."

Annuity companies are scrambling to offer products and strategies for the trillions of dollars of retirement money in motion. The annuity industry has not really changed much over the last few decades, but it is getting ready to change very soon, like it or not. As with all demographic tidal waves, the consumer eventually dictates the rules. Companies will fall in line with their demands in order to survive.

Simple and Transparent Products
The majority of annuities currently sold are very complex deferred variable or indexed annuities. A conspiracy theorist might say that's because those offer the agents the highest commissions. Let's hope that's not true. Another reason might be that annuity companies think that offering complex products with a myriad of add-on benefits—all those riders, as discussed in previous chapters—is what the public wants. They could not be more wrong about this "one-size-fits-all" approach.

In the very near future, the annuity buying consumer will demand simpler and more transparent products. I always tell people that if you cannot explain the annuity strategy to a nine-year-old, then you probably should not buy it. Future annuity products will be very easy to understand, simple, and involve no hoodwinking of the consumer.

Annuity Guarantees without Having to Buy an Annuity

Annuity is the curse word of the financial industry, a stigma well-earned because of the way that too many annuity products have been poorly explained, presented, and sold. Consumers still want contractual guarantees and benefits, but some just cannot stomach the possibility of owning an annuity. Even though I am Stan The Annuity Man, I fully understand that sentiment considering how annuities have been improperly hyped and sold in recent years.

A few companies that are starting to address this product void are now offering annuity type income guarantees that you can attach to a typical stock and bond portfolio. Technically, such a product is called a Contingent Deferred Annuity (see page 44), and it really functions as a stand-alone income guarantee with no surrender charges.

In essence, you can attach to your portfolio an income rider that will put a contractually guaranteed income stream in place as you continue to manage your assets. It is simply a fantastic idea, and I look forward to watching this product category grow. Currently, these products have many limitations from a structure standpoint, but I like the direction in which this category is moving.

Buying Annuities Directly

We all can remember when the online companies such as Schwab, Fidelity, and Vanguard came on the scene and started offering low-cost and direct solutions for stock, bonds, and mutual funds. At that time, I was working for one of the large Wall Street firms that somehow did not feel threatened by this new low-cost direct business model. Trillions of dollars later, it is an understatement to say that those online companies changed the financial game and the way people invest.

The same thing is going to happen in the annuity industry. Of course, the annuity czars vehemently disagree with me. They are obviously wrong. History will repeat itself once again, and most annuity offerings will be offered directly to the consumer in the very near future. The same predictable industry arguments will be voiced, only to be eventually shot down by those in charge—consumers.

Stanopsis: The Final Word

Annuities are not perfect products—there is no such thing. Annuities are neither one-size-fits-all nor too good to be true. However, annuities *are* fantastic contractual solutions that solve specific problems. Your situation is unique to you, so the annuity solution that I develop for you will be customized and tailor-made to contractually achieve your goals. Your own solution might involve just one annuity, or it might involve multiple annuities to contractually accomplish the task.

Remember the P.I.L.L.© acronym when deciding where and if an annuity might fit into your portfolio:

P rincipal Protection

I ncome for Life

L egacy

L ong-term Care

It might be time to transfer some risk to solve for those four goals. Ask yourself how much risk are you shouldering right now and how much of it you would like to transfer.

One more time: Remember to always purchase an annuity for what it *will do* (contractual guarantees), not what it *might do* (hypotheticals).

Contact me any time, and let's have a full discussion to see if an annuity strategy can complement your specific situation.

Sincerely,

Stan The Annuity Man®

PART II

STANDEX

Alphabetical Order

PART III

PLANET
ANNUITYMAN™

The AnnuityMan Steakhouse™: "All Steak...No Sizzle"

<hr />

As you know by now, I always advise people to "buy the steak, not the sizzle" when it comes to annuities. Some agents have a tendency to focus on a few positive bullet points without fully explaining the good, the bad, and the limitations of the product. All annuities have limitations, so you should know what they are.

Always make your decision to buy an annuity solely on the contractual guarantees. Never be influenced by hypothetical, theoretical, projected, or back-tested return scenarios. You want to own an annuity for what it will do, not what it might do. "Will do" is defined by the contractual guarantees.

So when you go to my "Annuity Steakhouse," your order should always be, "I'll have only the contractual guarantees please...nothing else." Hold firm to that request; do not budge or be influenced to modify your order. If you do that, you will be satisfied with the annuity strategy you decide upon.

Our motto at The AnnuityMan Steakhouse™ is "All Steak, *No Sizzle.*" It is the part of my website where we show actual examples of the vast majority of strategies I use and recommend for my clients. We constantly update the numbers to reflect current interest rates, current carrier contractual guarantees, and any new product offerings. You should plan on visiting The AnnuityMan Steakhouse™ every month to check out what's new on the "annuity menu."

Annuity quotes and products are constantly changing, so that is why you have not seen any illustrations and numbers listed in this book. I opened The AnnuityMan Steakhouse™ online to show up-to-date examples that always reflect current rates and annuity product offerings.

These numbers provide a realistic and timely look at what the annuity contractual guarantees would provide if implemented. I only show the contractual guarantees, which is all you should consider when buying an annuity. You are comparing based on what they *will do*, not might do.

Go to The AnnuityMan Steakhouse™ link on my website to see current numbers and to request a quote designed to fit your individual needs.

Schedule Stan The Annuity Man® to Speak

When it comes to annuities, I have been called the most controversial and entertaining speaker in the country. I can tailor my message to fit your organization, or you can choose from a list of topics that you feel would bring value to your group or membership.

My "Annuity Truth" presentations have become famous for stripping away all of the typical sales pitch nonsense. I know how to get right to the point of how annuities really work and where they should fit in a portfolio. You will not be disappointed if you bring me in to speak. That's a promise!

Contact our offices directly for pricing, scheduling, and travel coordination.

AnnuityMan™ Consulting Services

The fastest growing part of my business, my consulting services, continue to provide a one-of-a-kind value proposition to the financial industry. Because I have a true national client base, along with decades of retail experience in the financial services industry at all levels, I can provide unique insight that proves useful everywhere from a retiree's kitchen table to the corporate board room.

If your company is in the annuity business, wanting to get in the annuity business, or wanting to compete directly with annuities, I can help clarify and simplify your message and strategies to directly achieve your goals. I shoot straight and get to the point quickly. I do not play games. I just play for you to win.

Please contact me directly to discuss my fees, coordinate schedules, and begin the process of Stan The Annuity Man® helping your company or organization win—and win big.

Stan The Annuity Man® on Television and Radio

Currently, I am a monthly guest on numerous radio and television shows nationwide and am available for appearances as an annuity critic and expert. Please contact my office if you would like for Stan The Annuity Man® to be a part of your radio or television show.

The Annuity Critic™ Newsletter

Published electronically and e-mailed directly to you, The Annuity Critic™ newsletter has quickly become the must read for all things annuity. Packed with timely information and my Stanalysis© on what's relevant in the annuity world, my newsletter also lists my coming appearances, workshops, and webinar schedules. Go to my website to view past issues and sign up to receive The Annuity Critic™ newsletter.

AnnuityMan™ Merchandise

In addition to this book, *The Annuity Stanifesto,* I also offer unique and fun AnnuityMan™ logo clothing and merchandise available for purchase on my website. If you become a client, everything is *free*. If you are not a client, all of the merchandise is sold at cost. Merchandise is where my creative and artistic side comes out, and it has been amazing to see how popular some of these shirt and hat designs have become. In fact, some AnnuityMan™ shirt designs have reached pop culture status and are being sold in retail clothing stores across the country to people who probably have no clue what an annuity is and just like how the T-shirt looks. Incredible!

AnnuityMan™ Articles

At the time of this book's publishing, I am writing numerous national annuity columns per month, and those articles are listed, categorized, and constantly updated on my site for easy reference and viewing. If you would like Stan The Annuity Man® to write for your publication or blog, please contact our offices to coordinate topics and ongoing scheduling.

AnnuityMan™ Videos

I am constantly adding instructional videos to my website and even have my own Annuity Man YouTube channel as well.

Stan The Annuity Man® Protocols

When you decide to engage my services to see if an annuity fits you, I only ask one thing …put down your defenses, and let's have a professional conversation to see if a contractually guaranteed annuity strategy is right for you. It might be, and then again it might not be. I will tell you when it is not a good addition to your portfolio. I have no problem doing that.

I promise to shoot straight and be honest and professional throughout the process. That is your role as well. Don't play games, and all I ask is that you show the professional courtesy to respond to my personal e-mails and calls. There is nothing urgent in life except your health, so with any annuity solution I develop for you, the decision will be made on your terms and within your timeframe.

Stan The Annuity Man has clients in almost every state, so the majority of our interactions will be by phone or computer via screen sharing. I will get in the car or on a plane to come see you if need be, so just let me know how you would like to work together and what you are most comfortable with.

Stan The Annuity Man® Mobile Apps

I am proud to be the first independent annuity advisor in the United States to offer the public an Apple iPhone and iPad app that allows you to learn about annuities on your own and at your leisure. The good news is that my Stan The Annuity Man apps are *free* and continuously updated to provide the most up-to-date annuity information at your fingertips.

Website and Calculators

It is important to me that you learn about annuities and how they work on your own terms. My website, just like my mobile apps, allows you to run your own numbers based on your particular age and situation. Stan The Annuity Man uses a proprietary and customized quote system that will list the top contractually guaranteed numbers for your specific situation. All of these calculators and services are *free*, courtesy of Stan The Annuity Man!

Recommended Resources

I am a true student of pop culture and read and study constantly anything that has to do with annuities…and other stuff as well. Here's a current list of my top eclectic must read choices.

Must Read Books:

Pensionize Your Nest Egg

How to Use Product Allocation to Create a Guaranteed Income for Life
by Moshe Milevsky and Alexandra Macqueen

The 7 Most Important Equations for Your Retirement

The Fascinating People and Ideas Behind Planning Your Retirement Income
by Moshe Milevsky

The Advisor's Guide to Annuities
by John Olsen and Michael Kitces

Taxation and Suitability of Annuities
by John Olsen

Annuities for Dummies
by Kerry Pechter

Steve Jobs
by Walter Isaacson

Insanely Simple
The Obsession That Drives Apple's Success
by Ken Segall

Must View Websites:

**National Association of Insurance Commissioners |
www.naic.org**
Here you can find information about new legislation as well as
direct links to state insurance commissions' websites.

National Association of Fixed Annuities | www.nafa.com
An industry lobbying group dedicated to the understanding of
fixed annuities.

National Organization of Life and Health Guaranty Associations | www.nolhga.com

Here you can find out what your state guaranty is.

Bankrate.com | www.bankrate.com

BankRate.com has a ton of calculators and financial articles for consumers.

MarketWatch | www.marketwatch.com

A subsidiary of *The Wall Street Journal*, this website has hundreds of current articles about all aspects of personal finance. Check me out under the RetireMentors section.

FixedAnnuityFacts.org | www.fixedannuityfacts.org

This website is a good resource for information about fixed annuities in general and is overseen by the National Association of Fixed Annuities.

Tax and Legal Advice

Let me be very clear about this important topic. *No* advisor or agent should serve as your tax advisor in any capacity. You should always use your CPA and/or tax lawyer for clarification of all of your tax questions. I will work with your tax expert if need be to ensure that any complicated tax issues are covered properly. If an agent or advisor claims to be a tax expert, they better have the letters CPA or JD after their name. No exceptions!